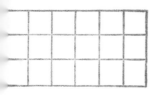

P9-DZO-737

LIBRARY

ONE FOR THE ROAD

ONE FOR THE ROAD

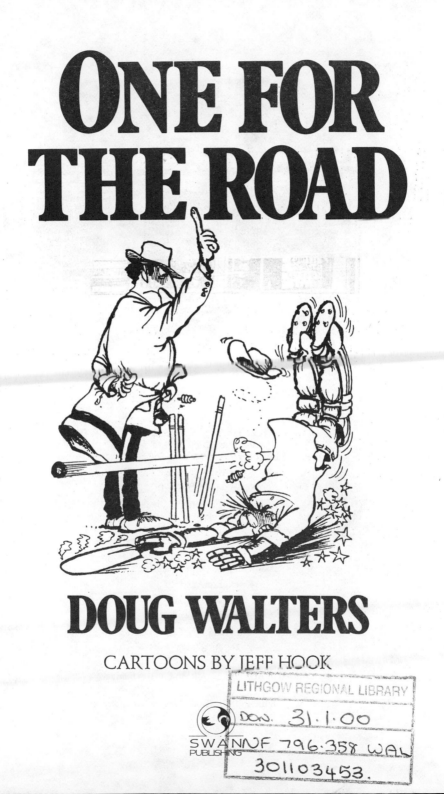

DOUG WALTERS

CARTOONS BY JEFF HOOK

Doug Walters

First published in 1988 by
Swan Publishing Pty Ltd
Level 1, 55 Lavender Street, Milsons Point, NSW 2060

Copyright © 1988

Swan Publishing Ltd

National Library of Australia
Cataloguing-in-Publication data.

Cricket in Australia

One for the Road

ISBN 0 9587841 3 2

1. Cricket — Australia. 2. Cricket Cartoons

798.35'8'0994

Typeset by Deblaere Typesetting Pty Ltd.
Printed in Australia by Griffin Press, Adelaide

Design: John Bull, The Book Design Company

CONTENTS

During my term as captain of Australia I often said I wouldn't want to tour without Doug Walters.

In part that was because of his exceptional skill as a batsman, his sneaky little medium-pacers that regularly broke partnerships and his brilliance in the field. But of equal importance to the team spirit was Doug's sense of humour and his delight in pulling off practical jokes.

Doug has a comedian's sense of timing. He will see or hear things and then store them away and use them when the moment is just right.

On the 1968 tour of England our manager Bob Parish was extremely fond of looking wistfully out of the team bus window at the lush green countryside and saying: "This is truly wonderful. Money can't buy this."

In 1977 Kerry Packer paid out millions of dollars to put together World Series Cricket. As the WSC Australians, we had our first meeting at the Melbourne airport. At the conclusion of the meeting we climbed aboard an Ansett bus and headed for the city. The suburb of Airport West in November isn't likely to be mistaken for Sanctuary Cove, with its dry, dusty paddocks and box-like houses surrounded by battered bikes and kids toys.

As our bus scooted along the freeway past this depressing sight, Doug puffed on a cigarette, looked out the window, and, without even a trace of a smile, muttered: "This is truly wonderful. But I must tell you Bob, money can buy it."

He'd waited a little over nine years to produce that gem, but judging by the laughter he'd chosen his moment perfectly.

Doug Walters is one of the truly great characters and I have no doubt they broke the mould when he was born. At least I hope they did, because I'd hate to be a young Australian cricketer trying to emulate Doug and finish with an average of 48 in a full Test career.

Doug has combined a successful sporting career with a good life. Despite living life to the full he's never let his mates down and has proved himself a good human being.

Reading through Doug's book the first thing that struck me was the way his effervescent character came through. The second thing was: "Boy, we had a good time, while still managing to play good cricket."

Through all the late nights and the practical jokes I still say: "I wouldn't want to go on a tour without Doug Walters."

I COULD DO NOTHING WRONG...!

1

A VERY SPECIAL SESSION

It took perhaps my finest two hours of cricket to really make me understand what mateship in the game was all about. And even then, my mates had a pretty bizarre way of showing it.

Those two hours were between tea and stumps at the WACA Ground in Perth in 1974 when I made a 100 against England. I hit the ball as well that day as I ever did. Certainly, it was one of only two occasions I 'did a Bradman' and made a Test century in a session.

I felt so good, so confident, that at one stage I had visions of being on 130 or so at stumps. My timing was sweet and so was my placement. I could do nothing wrong. I was on three at tea and in the 60s when drinks were taken at the halfway mark of the session.

Ross Edwards was my partner and, in the last hour, he tried his damndest, but without a great deal of success, to farm the strike my way. The more he tried, the more things ran in the opposite direction, and, at one stage I didn't face a ball in four or five overs.

I can't deny that a century in that session was very much in my mind once the foundation of the innings had been laid. I wasn't going to throw the bat at everything, but if there were 100 runs up for grabs, then I was going to grab them.

I was on 93 when Bob Willis started the last over, and Ross still had the strike. Not for long. He pushed the first ball away for a single, which left me seven deliveries (eight-ball overs in those good old days) in which to muster 10 runs.

Willis pitched the second ball short, I tried to hook and top-edged it over wicketkeeper Alan Knott's head. It (the ball, I mean, not Alan Knott's head) bounced a couple of times on its way to the sightscreen.

It was one of the few miscues of the innings, so I figured I didn't owe the Poms too much. Still we wouldn't let the blood rush to the head, would we, Doug? We'd go about this scientifically.

As the ball was retrieved and returned to Willis I figured I could expect one or two more short balls in the six remaining. He'd been averaging two or three an over so I decided to tackle the assignment on the back foot.

Sure, if I could pick up the six runs I needed by more conservative methods, I'd do it that way. But if it came to the crunch and the last ball was pitched short, I'd give it buggery. Balls three, four, five, six and seven were well up and on the stumps. No joy there. Okay. One to go, so if I was going to do this thing, I'd have to put it over the top.

I can imagine what was running through Willis' mind as he walked back to his distant mark. He'd pitch the ball short and really try me out. Would I be game enough to hook and risk holing out to either of the men he'd placed on the backward square-leg boundary? Or would I treat it with ignorance and shut up shop just six runs short of a magic, personal milestone.

Short it was, and hook I did. It was one of those times when bat hits ball at precisely the right moment. How sweet it was! The ball sailed away, neatly bisected the two guys out at backward square and thudded over the boundary. Six! You bloody beauty!

The crowd, who had buoyed me along for the previous hour, went bananas. They spilled onto the arena and slapped my back sore as I sought the sanctuary of the dressing room.

Ah yes, the dressing room. Now wouldn't that be a scene, I thought. The guys would mob me, they'd pump my hand, say "Bewdy Doug" and all that sort of stuff. They'd probably douse me with Champagne. I'd be a hero among my peers. I rather fancied that.

Surprise! When I walked into the room I found it empty. Not a soul in sight. You bastards, I thought. Here's a man hitting a six off the day's last ball to complete a century in a session and you haven't got the decency to be there to hero-worship me when I get back. You probably didn't even watch the last over. Where are you, you sods?

Surprise number two was when Ian Chappell appeared from a toilet-shower and gave me a blast. "You dopey bastard!" he said. "What do you mean by playing a totally irresponsible shot and getting out on the last ball of the day? Haven't you learned *anything* about team first, individual second?"

Jesus, that's lovely, I thought. Not only had he not *seen* the last over, but he'd stuffed up what happened anyway. 'Chappelli' glared at me for a couple of seconds. Then he broke into a huge grin and gave me a hug – the pre-arranged signal for the rest of the guys to emerge from hiding in the showers.

Sure they'd seen it, and what a reception they gave me! Doug Walters didn't have to open his own beers that night. That was all done for him. "Freddie, let me get you another drink"... "Well, okay, if you insist."

11

They must have whipped the tops óff a few too many for me because I was out second ball next day.

Still, a Test century in a session was really something – almost as memorable as the reaction from a great bunch of blokes in the dressing room.

Obviously, that innings rides high on my list of pleasant cricketing memories. Others that come readily to mind were against the West Indies, 242 and 103 in the Fifth Test in 1968/69 at the S.C.G. and 100 in a session in Trinidad in 1973, and 250 against New Zealand in Christchurch. But I mention that Christchurch innings only because it was a big score. It was not one of my best knocks. Put it this way: it was my worst double-century.

I made the first hundred on the first day of the match and Gary Gilmour was with me at stumps. We decided the century called for a bit of a celebration and Dick Tucker, a journo on the tour, didn't seem too impressed when he poked his head into the bar on his way upstairs to bed and saw 'Gus' and me holding a two-man party. Neither was Kerry O'Keeffe, who was next man in.

Kerry figured the shape we were going to be in next morning would not be conducive to an extended stay at the crease, so he was at the nets bright and early sharpening up his batting techniques in expectation of an early call to duty.

He needn't have bothered. 'Gus' went on to make a century and I saw it out to 250. It wasn't a bad effort for a morning-after-the-night-before but, as I said, I'd batted better.

Undoubtedly, the highlight of my career was my selection in 1965 to play for Australia for the first time. It was the dream fulfilled ... those boyhood thoughts of playing for your country, those fantasies you conjured up when you were in short pants and bashing a tennis ball against the side of the house.

That thrill of Test selection surpassed anything else that happened to me in cricket.

I'll never forget the first morning of that match, against England in Brisbane. I'd sort of convinced myself that I'd be 12th man and I couldn't really believe it when that job went to Alan Connolly. I felt sorry for Alan but elated that my big moment had come.

I like to think I made the most of it. I made 155 in the first innings, but the runs were merely a bonus. Disappointments? The biggest, I suppose, was my failure to make a Test century in England. I toured England four times and played some of my best cricket there. Yet I never cracked it for a Test hundred – a fact of which I am still consistently reminded. Three 80s were my best. A ton would have been very, very satisfying.

The plain, simple explanation is that my technique was not suited to English conditions in general and the slower English wickets in particular.

The other reason is that English cricketers devote more time to their homework than their counterparts elsewhere. They study every opponent, pick his weakness and dwell on it. They are prepared to bowl at that weakness all day.

In my case, 90 per cent of the balls they bowled at me were intended specifically to encourage shots in the direction of gully. I grew accustomed to three or four fieldsmen in the gully cordon every time I walked to the crease. A gully catch was my undoing more often than not. They are a crafty, dogged lot, the Poms.

Yes, a Test century in England would have topped it all off nicely, but cricket was very good to me and I thoroughly enjoyed my career. Given that career over, I wouldn't change a stroke of it.

2

AMOROUS, AMBIDEXTROUS JOE

Cricket was more a tradition than a boom sport when I was what you might loosely call an up-and-comer at Dungog, a country town 150 miles north of Sydney. I guess our local cricket team was typical for a bush town about our size. We had the bare 11 players, so you didn't have to bat like a Bradman or bowl like a Lindwall to get a game. It was a proud tradition, though, that as far as anyone could recall, Dungog had always fielded a full team (if you discounted the luxury of a twelfth man!)

We were down at the local one Saturday night celebrating another loss when, right on closing time, someone asked the captain who was taking Young Johnny's place for tomorrow's all-day game. Good question. Young Johnny had got himself married that very evening and was off on a fortnight's honeymoon.

The skipper pondered, shrugged and said: "There's no-one else in this town who plays cricket. We'll just have to play a man short."

Now that just wasn't on, tradition being what it was, and as alternatives were being tossed about the bar, someone suggested 'that bloke Joe from Sydney'. Joe had recently settled in Dungog and there was a suggestion that he had played a bit of cricket in the city.

So at five past 10 that Saturday night, the skipper phoned Joe. Could he help us out tomorrow?

"Cricket?" said Joe. "Gee, I dunno. I haven't played for four or five years. I'd be a bit rusty on it."

No worries, said the captain. "Up here in the bush we don't worry about things like that. As long as we have 11 men we won't embarrass ourselves by playing one short."

Okay, Joe would help us out, but where were we playing and what time were we starting?

At the local park: 10 o'clock start.

"Christ", said Joe, "10 o'clock on a Sunday morning's a bit early for me. I might be half an hour late."

Again, no worries. Turn up any time you like. She'll be right, Joe.

We arrived at the ground at 9.30 the following morning and there was Joe, in his creams, warming up, smashing the kids' bowling around the park. Looked a likely type, did Joe, and when his turn came to bat he went out, right-handed, made 50 not out and won the match for us.

We didn't win too many in those days and it was a lively night at the local, I can tell you. Just before closing time, the skipper approached Joe and said: "That was great mate, and we're going to need you again next Sunday because Young Johnny's still on his honeymoon. Can you help us out again?"

"Sure," said Joe. "I quite enjoyed that today. A bit of exercise and a few runs. Yeah, I'll be in it again. Where are you playing and what time?" Same place; same time.

"Not another one of those 10 o'clock starts!" Joe complained. "Bit early for me. I might be half an hour late."

Again no worries. Any time you like.

15

Joe beat us to the ground the following Sunday morning and was out there again, smashing the kids around the park, when we arrived. And when his turn came he went out, made 60 not out, left-handed, and won the match for us.

Fantastic! No-one could remember Dungog winning two in a row before and the local was fairly jumping that night. Ten o'clock came, the skipper walked up to Joe and said: "Absolutely great mate. We're not going to need you next week because Young Johnny'll be back from his honeymoon. But before you go, you've got us all puzzled.

"Last week, you batted right-handed and made 50 not out; today you batted left-handed and made 60 not out. You played just as well left-handed today as you did right-handed last week. So how do you decide which hand you're going to bat?"

"Well," said Joe, "you know all cricketers have their superstitions, but with me it's quite simple. It all depends on which side my wife is sleeping when I wake up in the morning.

"If she's sleeping on her right side, I say Joe, we'll bat right-handed today; if she's sleeping on her left side, I say Joe, we'll go left-handed today.

"And if she's sleeping on her back... I might be half an hour late."

16

3

A PUFF OR TWO, A PINT OR THREE

The drinking and smoking habits of Doug Walters have, I suppose, found themselves a little niche in modern cricket folklore. It's no secret that I enjoy a pint and a puff. I've never denied that I enjoy them – and you'll never find me practising my vices (ugly word) behind the woodshed or in the cupboard.

What you might not know, though, is that I was a bit of a late starter in both fields.

I was never a schoolboy smoker. Sure, I tried it, but a packet of fags would have comfortably seen me through my schooldays.

I was still a non-smoker when, at 20, I applied for a job at Rothmans. It certainly wasn't the lure of tobacco that took me along to that particular company.

It was their nice reputation for employing sportsmen and allowing them the necessary time off to pursue their respective games. I'd played one Test series at that stage – against England in 1965-66 – and I was looking for an employer sympathetic to my cricketing ambitions.

It got down to the final interview with Rothmans' NSW manager and he wasn't too upset when I told him I didn't smoke. "That doesn't worry us much provided you're willing to carry them on you and offer them around," he said. Fine by me.

SMOKE STARTED COMING OUT MY NOSE, MY EARS AND MY EYES!

I got the job and sat in the office for a couple of weeks reading sales letters and all sorts of things. I was called up for National Service within a few weeks of joining the company, but they managed to send me out on a few promotional jobs with Norm O'Neill, and some other guys from the promotions department, before I left to learn how to defend my country.

My first promotion was a matter of handing out Consulate menthol cigarettes at Sydney's Eastlakes shopping complex – and it should have turned me off smoking for life. The first bloke I offered a sample said: "They can't be too bloody good if you're not going to have one yourself."

I smiled like a good promotions man and said sure I'd have one with him. No sweat, I thought. I'd light up, have a couple of puffs and put it out as soon as I got rid of him and walked around the corner. So I lit up, and smoke started coming out of my nose, my ears and my eyes. I started to cough uncontrollably. Great advertisement for Consulate menthols, I was. The guy walked off laughing and I walked off spluttering. I wonder if he ever bought another packet.

The performance was repeated at other promos before I left to start 'Nashos' at Wagga. I really couldn't see myself ever becoming a smoker, but Rothmans sent me 1500 cigarettes a month and I became the most popular bloke in the Australian Army. I was handing out packets all over the place. Come to think of it, if I'd put the officers on my free list, I might have made Field Marshal.

One night, I got up in the boozer, where everyone was smoking my cigarettes, and said: "Give me one of those." And that was the smoke that did it.

I started bludging my own cigarettes back off these

guys, one or two a day at first, then more and more as the habit grew. By the end of my army days, Rothmans had jacked up my allowance to 2000 a month, and I was smoking the lot myself.

They reckon it shortens your life, but I can't imagine life – long, short or indifferent – without a cigarette.

I'd acquired a bit of a taste for a beer before I did National Service. It actually started at a most unlikely venue – a squash court. I was playing a lot of squash in those days, four times a week including two nights of the competitive stuff. Because I was a non-drinker our tour organizers put me on last, so they could finish their own games and slip into the amber while I was still out there on the court.

My game finished pretty late one night. It was a tough five-setter and when it was over I had a thirst that'd trip a camel. I was spitting sparks by the time I got back to the rooms – and there wasn't a soft drink to be had. No orange juice, no squash, no nothing. Except beer. Plenty of that.

So I downed a couple at a hundred miles an hour and decided it wasn't too bad. Another, if you please.

Yes, I like a beer and a smoke – and I've had a few of each since the squash club put me on to one and the army on to the other.

Tooheys' decision to sign me up for their 2.2 beer promotion was a logical extension of my well-known liking for a sip. I mean, they weren't going to ask a teetotaller to flog the product, were they! I'd never fancied myself as a TV star, but those commercials were great fun in the making. For one thing, my co-star was Maxie Walker – and he's about the best company you can get.

The first commercial was shot at the NSW Golf Club

21

at La Perouse and it called for Max to hook a ball into the deep rough.

MOJO, the advertising agency with the Tooheys contract, were very thorough and went to the trouble and expense of commissioning the club pro to teach Max how to hook. They needn't have bothered. Max is a natural hooker of a golf ball. Most blokes slice. Max Walker hooks. I reckon he hit 250 golf balls in the lead-up to the actual shoot and 248 of them took the same path – the hooker's path into the deep rough. Any one of them was just what the MOJO people wanted. I mentioned to one of the agency guys that what could have been achieved in a couple of minutes had taken all day and he said, "Oh well, that's showbiz." Whatever that means.

The other personally memorable Tooheys commercial called for Max and me to fall overboard while fishing. It was full of intangibles: would I drown? Would I be taken by a shark? Or would hypothermia get me? The commercial was shot on Sydney's Hawkesbury River in mid-winter, and, because my swimming season starts on January 1 and ends two days later, I considered the schedule to be all at sea.

I also have this unfortunate habit of doing all the wrong things when my head's under water. Like trying to breathe. They tell me that's not on.

On the way across in the boat, I noticed they'd brought along seven sets of gear for us and you didn't have to be psychic to deduce that this was going to be a seven-shoot session. The odds about drowning/shark attack/hypothermia were shortening by the minute.

I tried to kid the film crew by telling Max it was amazing what they could do with trick photography these days and chances were we wouldn't even get our feet wet. The crew just grinned and said they'd have news for us before the day was over.

We managed to reduce seven takes to just four – but Max nearly drowned me twice in the process. At one stage, his huge frame had me pinned on the bottom in 14 feet of water.

Next time I fall overboard with Max Walker, I'm going to insist on a stunt man.

It was always obvious to me that there was going to be life after cricket for Max Walker. Indications from way back were that the entertainment field, in some shape or form, was going to be his bag.

'Tangles' always had the gift of the gab and when you combined that with a natural and keen sense of humour, you knew he was going to be something more in retirement than a bit player on the sportsmen's night circuit. It doesn't surprise me at all that he is now a polished and very popular sports commentator on the Nine Network.

Maxie's comedy turns were often strictly ad lib . . . and I doubt he'll forget the First Test against the West Indies at Sabina Park, Kingston, in 1973.

Lawrence Rowe was giving us quite a pasting with the bat and Max, who was fielding on the fine-leg boundary, was the only Australian who seemed to be enjoying himself. He was playing to the crowd in his vicinity and they were responding with typical rum-spiked Caribbean enthusiasm.

The by-play had to be forgotten when Rowe hooked Dennis Lillee hard and high. 'Tangles' sprinted 30 yards around the boundary and pulled in a fantastic catch, rolling over and over before springing to his feet and holding the ball aloft to the section of the crowd he'd been entertaining for most of the day.

His great moment was absolutely ruined by skipper Ian Chappell, who tapped him on the shoulder and said: "For Christ sake, Maxie, throw it back. It was a no-ball and they've already run three!"

4

WHAT'S IN A NAME?

Every cricketer worth a bat or a bowl has a nickname. It applies at all levels, from international right down through the junior grades in the bush. A good thing, too, because it develops team spirit and recognises acceptance and belonging.

Nicknames have all sorts of origins, some obvious, some mighty obscure.

Rod 'Bacchus' Marsh was an obvious one, particularly to Victorians, who will tell you 'Bacchus' Marsh is a very pleasant town between Melbourne and Ballarat. It is doubly significant when you consider that Bacchus was the god of wine in Greek and Roman mythology and that Rodney has been known to taste the fruit of the vine on very special occasions.

My wife, Caroline, saw it in a different light after watching two of his first Tests, against England in Brisbane and Sydney in 1970. Those were games in which a nervous young wicketkeeper dropped catches and fumbled to the extent that the England camp dubbed him 'Iron Gloves'. Caroline asked, innocently and seriously, if 'Bacchus' was derived from "Back us up or there'll be more byes going through".

A more obscure tag was Dennis Lillee's 'FOT'. It became as much a part of Australian cricket as Dennis himself, yet I doubt that its origin has ever been publicly explained. 'FOT' dates back to Tony Lock's leadership of the Western Australian Sheffield Shield team. Here were two men of very strong personality and Lock would often get that little extra performance out of Dennis by telling him he was bowling like a 'f------ old tart'. Now that was quite a mouthful, and a little bit off-colour, too, to be tossing about every time you referred to Dennis. So it became simply 'FOT'. And didn't it stick!

Bill Lawry was 'The Phantom' for a reason other than any ghostly image his appearance, manner or batting

RUN FOR YOUR LIVES – IT'S THE GHOST WHO WALKS!

technique might have suggested. Bill was a non-smoker and while the other guys might be putting a few away in the bar, he'd be sitting in his room reading Phantom comics. It was as simple as that.

Ian Chappell was, and always will be, 'Chappelli', the I being appended to his name on the scoreboard to distinguish him from brother Greg. He was also known as 'Bertie' after someone suggested he attacked the bowling like Bert the Butcher.

Greg was known to the Queensland cricket fans as 'Handles' but only Queenslanders ever knew why. I always called him 'The Coke Man' because he worked for Coca-Cola in Adelaide. On the tour of the Caribbean, the boys likened his frizzy haircut to the head of a typical West Indian and called him 'Local'.

Kerry O'Keeffe was 'Skull' because of the close-cropped hairstyle of his younger days; Alan Turner was 'Fitteran', as in fitter and turner; and David Sincock was 'Evil Dick'.

Another obvious nickname was Max 'Tangles'

'TANGLES' IN ACTION !

27

Walker, for his tangle-footed bowling approach. Ashley Mallett was 'Rowdy' because it was difficult to get a word out of him, Jeff 'Two-Up' Thomson was named after the famous Thommo's two-up school in Sydney and certainly not for obscene gestures, and Ray Bright was a natural for 'Candles'.

Bruce Laird was 'Stumpy' because he stood not much above stump height; they took Ian Davis' initials and made him 'The Whizz' (after the Wizard of Id); Graham Corling was 'I'llbe' (I'll be calling you...); and Gary Cosier was 'Jaffa' (short for Jaffa Head, a comparison with his hair colour and those orange lollies some people probably still roll down the aisles of uncarpeted picture theatres).

Johnny Martin was 'The Favourite'. He was introduced to a chap one day who said, "I'm delighted to meet you, you've always been a favourite of mine." It was actually a very appropriate nickname because Johnny is a great guy and a lot of people's favourite.

Jim Higgs was always 'Glad', short for Glad Bags. When he started at grade level in Melbourne, Jimmy didn't have a cricket bag – or if he did, he didn't use it. He'd turn up at the ground with his gear in Glad Bags.

I was responsible for Brian 'Herbie' Taber. I knew his initials were H.B. and after pondering it one day, I decided the 'H' must stand for Herbert. So Herbie it was. I learned a little later it was, in fact, Headley Brian Taber, but Herbie seemed to fit the personality and that's how it stayed.

Johnny Gleeson earned 'CHO' on a tour of New Zealand. Johnny was rarely seen by the rest of the touring party outside playing hours. He'd disappear at the end of the day's play and reappear in the dressing room next morning. He became 'CHO' because he was seen during Cricket Hours Only.

Peter Toohey was 'Rats'. Not a particularly endearing nickname, and it had nothing to do with his appearance or personality. Someone remarked when Peter was rolling his arm over in the nets one day that he looked like he was trying to bowl rats out of a drainpipe. So 'Rats' it was.

I was 'Little Dougle' who became 'Biki' who became 'Freddie'. And thereby hangs a bit of a tale.

Doug Ford was keeping wicket for New South Wales when I made the Sheffield Shield team and when you have two blokes with the same Christian name in the same team, you have a recipe for a certain amount of confusion. And when those two blokes are given the same nickname, you are courting chaos.

Doug (Ford, that is) had long been known as 'Little Dougle' – which was fair enough because he was nearer four foot eight than eight foot four. When diminutive Doug from Dungog joined the ranks, I was given the same tag. I thought at the time they might have shown a little more imagination and flair, but when you're a kid thrown in among guys you've hero-worshipped for years, you don't mention things like that.

Every time 'Little Dougle' was mentioned in the dressing room, we'd both respond.

"No, not *you*, Little Dougle," someone would say, "I mean *that* Little Dougle over in *that* corner."

Pretty soon, it became... "no, I mean Tiny Little Dougle, over *there*."

Little Dougle (being Doug Ford) started answering to Tiny Little Dougle... "not *you*, Tiny Little Dougle, I mean Itsy Bitsy Tiny Little Dougle."

The whole thing was getting out of hand. We were both answering to whatever anyone happened to put in

29

front of 'Dougle'. And we were getting smaller all the time. We started to realise how the Incredible Shrinking Man must have felt.

There was a song called Itsy Bitsy Teeny Weeny Yellow Polka Dot Bikini on the hit parade at that time and Peter Philpott, one of the senior and most respected members of the NSW team, drew a parallel as he pointed out the dangerous direction in which this nickname farce was heading.

"Look," he said, "what happens if Doug (Walters) is fielding in slips, there's a fly ball off the edge and you're both going for the catch?

"The rest of us haven't got time to yell, it's yours, Itsy Bitsy Teeny Weeny Yellow Polka Dot Bikini, not yours, Tiny Little Microscopic Dougle.

"Christ, by the time you've worked out who's who, the ball will be on the ground and the batsmen will have run seven!

"Let's take Bikini, drop the last couple of letters and call him 'Biki'."

Okay, they said, but which one?

"Tiny Little Dougles, you stupid bastards," said Peter. "Little Dougles was here first!"

There was a fleeting danger the situation could get out of control again. But 'Biki' it was for Doug Walters, and 'Biki' it stayed until Ian Redpath, in a rare irrational moment, came up with 'Freddie'. 'Redders' saw a similarity between the way Freddie Trueman and I ran in to bowl.

If he was being fair dinkum, the resemblance stopped there. I mean, Trueman lacked my pace, my ability to swing the ball either way and my lethal bouncer!

I had no objection to 'Biki' but, given the choice, I'd cop 'Freddie' any old time. It made me feel taller.

5

BEERS...THEN CHEERS

The South Africans who beat the Australian tourists 4-0 in the 1970 series were the second-best cricket team I played against. The best was any of a number of the West Indian sides which so dominated international cricket in the decade up to the mid-1980s. It's impossible to nominate any of those Windies sides as *the* best because they were all so good. You could take your pick.

That 1970 South African combination was top class and we were done like so many dinners. It had been a long tour, taking in Ceylon and India along the way, and it was almost a relief when the Springboks had completed their whitewash of us. We'd been away almost six months yet after the final Test we still had two games to go before we were on our way home. I knew I was going to have the last game off but in the meantime I had an appointment in the match starting in Cape Town the day after the Test.

I'd been rooming with Brian Taber all tour and we used to take it in turns ordering breakfast each night before we went to bed. 'Surprise Breakfasts' we called them because the other bloke had no idea what he was getting until hotel room service knocked on the door.

We'd been out until the small hours celebrating our Test losses and didn't seem to get much sleep at all –

31

which was naughty of us, I guess, bearing in mind that we had to front for the first of those two remaining tour matches. It had been Brian's turn to order breakfast and when the tap on the door woke me about 8 a.m., I said: "Okay, mate – you know the rules. Whoever orders breakfast lets them in."

Boy, was *this* a surprise breakfast! Six bottles of beer on a tray!

Brian had anticipated that a hair of the dog might be just what we needed at that hour of the morning, and after what we'd been through the night before, I tended to agree. So we sat on the edge of the bed and downed them.

By the time we'd showered and dressed it must have been right on the dot of 10 a.m. because on the way downstairs there was a bloke lifting the shutters on the first-floor bar and announcing that he was open for business.

Brian was three or four paces ahead of me and he stuck his head under the ascending shutters and said: "Two beers please, pal." 'Tabsy', I said, we've got to get to the ground (which was five or six miles away), but he pointed out that the team taxis had left half an hour ago, that he had a car and knew the way to the ground, so no worries.

Okay. So we took the first sip of that cold draught beer and agreed it tasted damned nice after the six warm bottles we'd just knocked over upstairs. And being a guy who likes to shout in turn, I said to the bloke: "We'd better have another couple of those."

Play was to start that day at 11 a.m. and we arrived at the ground, feeling much better thank you very much, with 10 minutes to spare. It was an enormous relief personally to see Bill Lawry padded up because that

meant he'd won the toss. And because I batted at No. 5 or 6 in those days it meant I'd have plenty of time to collect my thoughts after that liquid breakfast. I mentioned that quietly to Brian, who shrugged and said: "No worry to me – I'm twelfth man today." Twelfth man! Now he tells me!

The morning had already bèen full of surprises, but Lawry had another one for me. "Oh Doug," he said, on his way out to open our innings, "it's your last game over here, so you can bat No. 3 today." He wouldn't have made that decision had he known what I'd just had for, and after, breakfast, but I didn't fancy saying, look skipper, I've had a bit of a morning skinful, do you mind if I give first drop a bit of a miss on this particular occasion?

No, that would never have done. So I settled for a "thanks very much, Bill." Then I looked straight at Keith Stackpole, who was opening with Bill, and said: "Stacky, you'd better keep your head down today." I didn't figure there was any sense in telling Bill to do that.

I'd just scrambled into my creams and donned the pads when a roar from the crowd told me just what I didn't want to know: someone was out, and the innings was only five minutes old.

'Stacky' had gone, and hadn't I told him to keep his head down? The whole thing was starting to shape up like a conspiracy.

So there I am, standing out in the middle of the Newlands Ground in Cape Town trying to find Mike Proctor. I know he's somewhere down by the sight screen at the other end, but I can't quite make him out. And I'm wondering how clearly I'm going to see him when he unleashes the first thunderbolt and if I'm going to see the first ball at all.

I'm wondering all sorts of things, but most of all I'm wondering what I'm going to say to Brian Taber when I get him alone. And I'm wondering what I'm going to tell my grandkids when they ask me: "Pop, how come you were clean-bowled first ball in your last game of the tour of South Africa in 1970?"

In retrospect, I should have been telling myself a few quiet beers never hurt anyone, did they? Because I made a ton that day – my only century of the South African trip.

6

'ROWDY'S' LITTLE MATE

Anyone who ever played cricket with Ashley Mallett could write a book about the bloke, his adventures and misadventures.

To you out there on the other side of the pickets 'Rowdy' might not have come across as one of the game's great characters. But spend time with him on the field, in the dressing room, and, particularly on tour, and you very quickly became aware that this was no ordinary man.

'Rowdy's' outstanding characteristic was his clumsiness. Ian Chappell has described him as the clumsiest cricketer of his experience, and that goes for me too. Ashley was a walking disaster area. He found it hard to negotiate the length of a room without knocking over a couple of tables or chairs.

He was incredible, yet the same fellow was one of the finest gully fieldsmen I have ever seen. You marvelled that a bloke devoid of co-ordination off the field could consistently pull in those blinding catches in perhaps the most difficult of all field positions. A considerable enigma was Ashley Mallett. He was also a sucker for the practical joke – which made him a regular target for just that!

I learned early in our association that 'Rowdy' had a thing about insects. Tell him there was a fly on his shoulder and he'd freak out; just mention the word 'spider' and he'd turn ashen. (Before the lepidopterists howl me down here and point out that a spider isn't an insect, let me say yes, I know. For one thing, it has a couple of excess legs, but that didn't matter to Ashley. To him any creepy-crawlie was an insect and, therefore, the enemy).

To make life more interesting for 'Rowdy', I bought him an imitation spider, a nasty-looking black rubber job, from a novelty shop and it was often in my pocket when we took the field.

... I'D STICK MY SPIDER TO THE BALL BEFORE I TOSSED IT TO ROWDY !

Out there I'd chew gum constantly, smoking being barred, and periodically I'd use a well-worn piece of it to stick my spider to the ball before tossing it to 'Rowdy' as he walked back to his bowling mark.

His reaction never varied. Suddenly aware of the dreaded foreign body, he'd hurl the lot, ball, gum and spider, into the outfield like an unpinned grenade. You'd have thought, after umpteen performances, that 'Rowdy' would have woken up to my little prank. He never did. I'll bet the crowd wondered what the hell was going on.

Then there was the old 'hot foot' gag. 'Rowdy' was a creature of habit and one of those habits was to kick off his boots and peel off his socks after a day's play and walk around the dressing room barefoot. The smokers among us didn't even have to aim our butts in his direction. You could be sure he'd tread on them eventually.

'Rowdy' liked a cigarette himself, but preferred not to buy them unless it was absolutely necessary. Not that there was any shortage of 'freebie fags'. The Benson and Hedges Company was a major sponsor of cricket and was more than generous with its product, but, because I was working for Rothmans in those days, 'Rowdy' regarded me as particularly fair game. I'd leave a packet of cigarettes on the table when I went out to bat and, depending on the length of the innings, it would be empty, or damn near to it when I returned.

The situation drove me back to the novelty shop. Miniature fireworks turned out to be a most effective deterrent. Pushed into the end of a cigarette, the firework would explode, quite harmlessly I hasten to add, after three or four puffs, and quickly turn Ashley off my brand of smoke!

'I QUICKLY TURNED ASHLEY OFF MY BRAND OF SMOKE!!'

I've mentioned Ashley's aversion to insects and I can add that he was no great shakes with snakes, either. We were being lavishly entertained at a party thrown by a Rajah in Bangalore during the 1969 tour of India when an eccentric, middle-aged Russian woman burst into the room and announced: "Hello. I'm Tanya – and I'm here!"

Eccentric? Well, the monstrous python draped around her neck tended to give her away. We had a chat with Tanya and decided she was just the girl to make 'Rowdy's' night. He co-operated too, to the point of dancing with the lady and even stroking the couple of visible coils of python. He gave us a smug, hey-fellers-cop-this-lot look as he tripped in the light fantastic.

It was when the python drew its head from somewhere within Tanya's ensemble and gave him the bare-fanged evil eye that 'Rowdy' went to water. He

... IT WAS WHEN THE PYTHON DREW ITS HEAD FROM SOMEWHERE WITHIN TANYA'S ENSEMBLE ...

reeled back aghast, flung his partner the length of the room – and bolted. For Ashley Mallett, that particular party was over.

Thanks to a most unlikely fan in a most unlikely place, 'Rowdy' became the central figure in the most hilarious sequence of events I have seen on a cricket field. Australia's tour of Ceylon (as Sri Lanka was then known), India and South Africa in 1969-70 was my first trip to that part of the world, and, the veterans of the party had some words of advice for we rookies – particularly about India.

"Don't drink the water," they said, which was okay by me. "The food's ordinary unless you moonlight as a fire-eater at the local circus, the accommodation's lousy, the crowds riot at the drop of a turban – and never, but *never*, get hit on the pad ... "

The pad warning was still fresh in the mind when we arrived at Jallundah to play North Zone. After what we'd been told about Indian umpires, it threw us a bit to find the two appointed for this game introducing themselves as we filed off the bus.

I can still see one of them, a little guy, shaking our hands, beaming and saying how honoured he was to be umpiring this cricket match because it was his first. We all took that to mean his first *international* match. But the events which followed led us to believe we'd got it wrong: when he'd said "first", he'd meant just that!

'Rowdy' followed me off the bus and into the clutches of this little umpire – who turned out to be a one-man Ashley Mallett Fan Club. "Ah, Mr Mallett," he said. "Mr Mallett . . . my goodness, I am so delighted to shake the hand of such a great spin bowler. My goodness me I am!"

He sounded a bit like a caricature of Peter Sellers as he reminded 'Rowdy' of just about every wicket he'd taken since he first played grade cricket in Perth. The little guy was amazing. He knew Ashley's career figures, average, best match figures – the lot. You name it. This bloke could.

'Rowdy' was never averse to a bit of flattery and half an hour later, as the umpire carried his hero's bags to the dressing room, statistics were still being bandied about, with false modesty on one hand and undisguised adulation on the other.

We thought it was nice for 'Rowdy' to have found such a friend. I don't have to tell you that wickets in India are prepared to spin at right-angles from ball number one and, having lost the toss, Bill Lawry put our opening quicks through the mandatory one over apiece before tossing the ball to Ashley. "Hey, 'Rowdy'," he said, "you'd better have a bowl from your mate's end."

Ashley's first four balls were pitched so wide of the off stump and spun so wide of the leg stump that the little

40

Indian opener couldn't have reached them with a tennis racquet on an extendable broomhandle.

So the batsman figured, quite reasonably, that if he wasn't going to be able to read or reach the prodigious spin, the way to go here was to step down the wicket and catch this man Mallett on the full, or on the half-volley. Yes, that would fix him. My word it would.

As 'Rowdy' ran in to bowl the fifth ball, the batsman ran seven or eight paces down the wicket. 'Rowdy' saw him coming. You don't have to be a genius with 20-20 vision to see him coming, but a lesser bowler might have stopped and wondered what the hell this was all about.

'Rowdy' merely tossed the ball higher, shorter and a little wider than the preceding deliveries. The ball spun back and hit the aggressive Indian on the pads. Ashley was known in the cricketing world as a bowler who would never die wondering if a batsman would have been given out. A John Bracewell type.

So he appealed. No-one else appealed. Just 'Rowdy'. It ranked among the more fatuous appeals I have seen – but 'Rowdy's' little white-hatted, bag-carrying mate said "out". Leg before wicket. Out? When the batsman's halfway down the wicket and the wicket's turning faster than a catherine wheel? How can that be out?

Only the umpire knew. We were embarrassed and even 'Rowdy' looked a little ashamed. The batsman merely stood there in a state of minor shock. But the umpire had no doubt. He raised and lowered his finger yo-yo fashion (as is the Indian custom) until his arm tired. He'd given him out so many times I think he'd mesmerised him.

And having done that he decided to come over to mid-off and have a chat with me. He tapped me on the shoulder and said: "Oh, this Mr Mallett, he's a very, very

41

fine bowler, this Mr Mallett." I said he wasn't a bad bowler as off-spinners go, but I thought the batsman had been a trifle unlucky.

"Oh no," said the umpire, "that was a very, very fine leg-break – that was a leg-break, that one." Okay, so where did we go from here?

Well, by that time, the No. 3 batsman had arrived in the middle, leaving his luckless predecessor no choice but to vacate the arena. Number three had obviously been studying proceedings from the dressing room and he figured the only mistake the previous batsman had made was not getting far enough down the wicket to catch this Mr Mallett on the full or half-volley. But he'd fix that.

It was the sixth and final ball of the over and Ashley and the new batsman commenced their runs at the same time. They met somewhere around centre wicket. Again, 'Rowdy' had seen him coming and tossed the ball

THEY MET SOMEWHERE ABOUT CENTRE WICKET!

higher, shorter and so wide I reckon it came off the wicket next door. And, sure enough, it spun back immensely and rapped the pads.

Brimful of confidence now after the result of the previous appeal, 'Rowdy' screamed the question at his little mate, who said: "Yes, that's out, too!" Then he strode back to me at mid-off and said: "I told you this Mr Mallett is a very fine bowler, didn't I?"

The situation was fast degenerating into pure farce and Bill Lawry wisely decided to separate 'Rowdy' and his bosom buddy. He banished Ashley to the other end and brought on Johnny Gleeson, the other spinner in our touring party. If he hadn't, the Indians might have been all out for four or five before lunch.

Johnny bowled five or six overs without hitting a pad at all, but managed to find the edge of a bat and wicket-keeper Brian Taber accepted the catch. It was a definite snick and there was no doubt the batsman was out, legitimately, fair and square. We all appealed, not a troubled conscience among us!

Amazingly, the same umpire who'd just 'murdered' two innocent batsmen gave no response. He stood there, as if meditating, for what seemed to us to be a couple of minutes, neither raising the finger nor shaking the head.

The suspense eventually overcame Johnny, who turned back to the umpire and demanded: "Well, is he or isn't he?" 'Rowdy's' little pal hesitated for 10 or 15 seconds, lifted the finger and said: "Yes, he's out."

Johnny bowled out the over and as the umpire handed him his cap, he said: "Oh, Mr Gleeson, I'm very, very sorry in taking so long to give that fellow out. But the wind was blowing in the opposite direction and it took quite some time for the snick to reach me down this end."

7

UNDERARM ICE-BREAKERS

I've seen a lot of joy and a lot of despair in various dressing rooms after various games of cricket in various countries. I've seen guys do outrageous things after a win; and I've seen them cry and turn into vandals after a defeat. Quite unique, though, was the atmosphere in the Australian room at the MCG after the famous (or infamous) underarm incident in the one-day final against New Zealand on February 1, 1981.

That last-ball grubber Greg Chappell ordered brother Trevor to bowl to give us a six-run win became the most discussed incident in modern cricket history. Compared with it, the kick in the pants Dennis Lillee gave Javed Miandad in Perth in 1981 was a routine, everyday event. Actually, I know a lot of people who thought Javed should have been kicked in the bum years before Dennis was moved to do it.

But getting back to the post-underarm dressing room atmosphere, I suppose the best word to describe it is 'eerie'. It had been a great game of cricket, right up to that last ball, and the huge MCG crowd had hung on every delivery, every stroke, every run.

Back in the room, we sat there in total silence, heads in hands or between knees. Win, lose or draw, Australian cricketers of my experience had always walked into the dressing room and made a beeline for the fridge. This time, not a beer was sought or produced. And not a word was spoken.

Was this an international cricket team after winning a major match? Or was this medidation hour in a Trappist monastery? Someone had to break the silence, and why not Doug Walters?

"Well, Greg," I said, "you've just destroyed my faith in one of the great stories on cricket. I was always led to believe that a game was never over until the last ball was bowled – and I haven't seen it yet."

The room didn't exactly erupt into laughter, but there was a series of chuckles so I figured I'd broken the ice. We all knew, though, that we were going to hear a lot more about that underarm delivery!

We were to play New Zealand again in the fourth, and deciding, final in Sydney two days later, and the arrangement was that the NSW guys in the team would fly home after the Melbourne game and the rest of the party would follow next morning. Greg decided he'd like to get out of Melbourne as soon as possible – and you couldn't blame him for that – so he came along with the NSW contingent.

We were among the last people to board the Sydney flight, and it was immediately obvious that everyone else on it knew who we were and what had happened at the MCG a few hours earlier. It was like our dressing room all over again: dead silence. In those days, they had a little tractor-type thing that towed the plane backwards away from the terminal and we slid soundlessly towards the runway. I reckon it was the quietest departure in aviation history.

"Greg," I said, "I knew we were trying to sneak out of Melbourne but this is ridiculous!" The remark wasn't intended for general consumption, but every passenger broke up.

A few years later, I was working with Trevor Chappell in a travel venture and the situation called for one of us to go to New Zealand on a business trip. I'd just done a trip to Bali, so I figured it was Trevor's turn. I had lingering doubts, however, about the reception he might get across the Tasman from Kiwis with long memories.

"Wanna go to New Zealand, mate?" I asked.

"Sure, I'd like that," he replied.

"Hang on," I said, "remember what happened in Melbourne in 1981? I hear the Kiwis mightn't have forgiven you and Greg yet. You might cop a bit of flak over there."

"Not half as much as I cop over here," he said. "Everywhere I go in Australia, people still ask me how my underarm's going."

So off he went and returned all smiles 10 days later.

"How did you go?" I asked.

"Bloody marvellous," said Trevor. "Only heard the word 'underarm' twice – and one of those was in a TV commercial for deodorant!"

8

OLD DOUG DIPS OUT

When the Australian selectors left me out of the 1981 tour of England, they must have been thinking along the same lines as a couple of blokes I'd just met in north Queensland.

I was doing a spot of coaching at Mackay and if you've ever been there in summer, you'll agree that it gets mighty hot. So hot that after the first coaching session I had to run down to the local for a quick lemonade at the bar. I was standing there minding my own business when an old guy walked in. He looked about 95 to me and he recognised me immediately.

"Doug Walters!" he said. "I've been dying to meet you." And he looked as if he was, as well.

As we shook hands, he said: "I've got a photo of you at home. It was taken a long time ago. You were only 15 at the time – 1930 that photo was taken!"

I didn't offer a shot at that one – but there was worse to come. A couple of days later, another bloke accused me of playing against Douglas Jardine's team in the 1932 Bodyline series! So I guess the national selectors were right in giving my place in the 1981 touring party to a younger man.

I wasn't too disappointed, from a cricket viewpoint, in missing that England tour because I'd been there and done that four times before. But for a couple of other reasons, I was quite put out.

For one thing, it denied me a chance of setting an in-flight can consumption record from Sydney to London that even Rodney Marsh would have found unbeatable.

For another, I missed out on the 500/1 odds they got about England beating Australia in that remarkable Third Test, at Leeds. Marshie and Dennis Lillee at first denied taking those odds – and you couldn't really blame them when people were being absurd enough to suggest they ran dead after putting the money on. But no way could Dennis or Rod, or the entire Australian team for that matter, deny betting on a game of cricket, also in England, in 1972.

Tour games against Yorkshire were traditionally very good contests and Ladbrokes, the famous English book-makers, thought enough of the 1972 fixture to depart from their cricket policy of only betting on Test matches. For the first time, they set up their tent for a non-Test occasion – and they'd barely pegged the thing down before the rains came. When the first of the three days was washed out without a ball bowled, the county officials got their heads together with our management and decided that two one-day games would be a much more satisfactory arrangement than one two-day match.

It meant reselecting our side – one day cricket being a different ball game – and because Dennis had already done a lot of bowling on the tour, Ian Chappell and his co-selectors decided he might like to carry the drinks in the first fixture.

Ian won the toss and invited Yorkshire to bat on a wicket still damp from the previous day's rain. It wasn't a very friendly wicket at all and we had them 4/40 after an hour with Geoff Boycott, playing a typically stubborn (dour might be a better word) innings, the only stumbling block on the immediate horizon.

I was fielding at fine leg, about a long-hop away from the Ladbrokes' tent, and I just happened to see Dennis emerge. I beckoned him over to the fence and said: "Made something favourite, have you Dennis?"

"No," he replied, "but I'm about to. You guys are 12/1 about getting five wickets in this session."

I did a quick double-take, consulted the scoreboard and the clock and decided that 12/1 – with just one wicket required and 90 minutes to go before lunch – was too good to be true. "There just happens to be 20 quid in my trouser pocket in the dressing room, mate," I said. "You'd better slip that on as well."

At the end of the over I thought, gee, wouldn't that little fat bloke with the wicketkeeping gloves on like to know what's happening in the betting tent. So as we changed ends I strode over and told him what was going on. Rodney Marsh didn't bother to look at the clock or the scoreboard – he has a mind like a steel trap when he thinks he hears the ring of a cash register – and promptly ordered 20 of the same.

Then there was Ian Chappell, who wandered down the wicket to see what match tactics Bacchus and I were discussing. He glanced casually at the scoreboard and asked to be written in for 20.

Then there was Ian's brother Greg. Should we tell him, too? Why not? Greg was always a deal more conservative than Ian and he took two looks at the clock and two at the scoreboard before he joined the punters' club. We knew he wasn't as confident as the rest of us. He limited his bet to 15 quid.

You'd be amazed how fast word can spread on a cricket field. By the time the first ball of the next over was

50

bowled, third-man wanted 20 and mid-on weighed in at 10. Deep backward square nominated for 20 after the next ball and by over's end everyone wanted a piece of the action.

I got back to fine-leg in time to see Dennis walking towards the Ladbrokes tent with his 20 and mine. 'FOT,' I said, "you'd better get some more money because the other boys want an interest in this as well."

Dennis always was an obliging guy and the money was duly found and invested. He gave us the thumbs-up sign from the fence. All bets on. Now it was up to us. You've never seen 11 blokes more intent on getting a wicket.

Success came 35 minutes before lunch – and in the most satisfying way. The identity of the bowler escapes me – and I put that down to the heady atmosphere of new-found riches – but whoever he was, he was quick and he sent Boycott's middle stump cartwheeling out of the ground. It was always great to see the end of Geoff Boycott. With a quid involved, the rewarding experience was multiplied.

Eleven blokes appealed vigorously, pretty rare when a batsman is comprehensively bowled. The dismissal was self-evident, but this time we were making sure.

Yorkshire went to lunch at 6/62, Ashley Mallett having taken one of his routine freak catches in the gully just before the adjournment. And we were on good terms with ourselves, doing our 12-times table as we left the field.

I told you Dennis Lillee was an obliging guy. He even interrupted his lunch to return to the Ladbrokes' tent to pick up our winnings. Oh happy days!

He was back a few minutes later with some chilling words: "I've got bad news for you boys."

Bad news? How could a 12/1 winner be bad news?

"That's it," he said. "It's about the bet."

"Oh no," said I. "You told me it was 12/1 about getting five wickets in the session. Well, we did better than that – we got six!"

"And that's where you made your mistake," Dennis said. "The bet was for five wickets – not six."

Lunch turned immediately sour and we sat there like million-dollar punters who'd just lost their all on an upheld protest or a jockey who'd weighed in light.

It took us a few beers after play that day to forgive 'Rowdy' Mallett for taking that sensational catch that had put us over the limit.

The episode taught me two valuable lessons: always read the fine print. And if someone mentions the glorious uncertainty of cricket, you'd better believe him!

The day after that team for the 1981 tour of England was announced, I was driving from Sydney to Newcastle to speak at a dinner. My wife Caroline and my son Brynley were with me. The morning papers and the radio news bulletins had not missed the fact that I was not going to England this time. Neither had it escaped the attention of Brynley, who was four years old.

We were about halfway to Newcastle when he said: "Hey Dad, where's that black bag of yours? That one you've always got in the back of the car with your cricket gear in it?"

"I'm not going to play cricket in Newcastle, mate," I replied. "I'm just going to talk at a dinner."

"Oh," said Brynley, "won't they let you play in Australia either now, Dad?"

I said before that the decision to leave me home in 1981 didn't break my heart. England wasn't my favourite country to tour and I think that's reflected in

my performances there.

In fact, it was during the 1972 tour that Tooheys first came up with the suggestion that they name their new beer after my batting average.

Yeah, 2.2 – and even that may have been flattering.

I was going so badly on that trip that my mother phoned from Australia during the Second Test at Lord's to give me some batting advice. The boys answered the phone in the dressing room and said no, she couldn't speak to Doug because he was out in the middle batting. She figured I wouldn't be long and said she'd hold on.

How right she was! It was just another three-minute call.

9

THE WIDE WORLD OF 'THE WOK'

I think back on all the cricketers I've played with and against and the name Johnny Watkins keeps bobbing up. Johnny who? you might ask. Johnny Watkins.

'The Wok' Watkins will not be remembered for illustrious cricketing deeds. In fact, his Test career was very much a here-today, gone-tomorrow affair. He was the NSW leg-spinner who was the shock selection for Australia's tour of the West Indies in 1973.

The nearest parallel I can draw to Johnny's selection is that of NSW off-spinner Peter Taylor for his Test debut against England in 1986. Both were unknown internationally and known very little domestically. But whereas Taylor bowled accurately and was an instant success, Watkins bowled unbelievably wide and was an unqualified failure.

I've never seen a player perform so well in the nets and so badly on the field as 'Wok'. In the nets, he could consistently drop the ball on a threepenny piece; but out there in the middle, he'd start off bowling wide and the more he bowled the wider he bowled. The wicket just wasn't wide enough for 'The Wok'.

No, it certainly wasn't his spinning prowess which keeps bringing his name back to mind. It's the fact that he was a character who didn't even know it.

The Australian selectors must have chosen Johnny for that 1973 Caribbean tour on his practice-net form alone. Maybe they saw him as a secret weapon. Certainly, they must have picked the team before they saw him bowl in the last Test against Pakistan, the series which preceded the West Indies tour. The game was in Sydney, it was his maiden Test and there were two strips out there. One was the Test wicket; the other, next door, had been prepared for a Sheffield Shield match the following week.

Did I mention that 'Wok' tended to bowl wide? You'd have sworn he was deliberately using the Shield strip in that Test. I reckon he hit it more often than the Test wicket he was supposed to be bowling on.

Johnny became a national hero in that match in the most unlikely way. If he wasn't much of a bowler, he was a handy batsman – he saved Australia by making 36 in the second innings. Thanks to his knock, we made just enough to scrape home when Max Walker and Dennis Lillee bowled Pakistan out for just 106.

I got along very well with 'Wok' on the tour of the West Indies. He must have heard a lot of untrue things about me, because he seemed to respect me. He was a nice guy who was also very gullible.

During the First Test, at Sabina Park in Kingston, Jamaica, he'd run six or seven laps of the ground at the end of each day's play. When I asked why, he said he was trying to keep fit for all the drinking he was doing on the tour. He was training more for his drinking than for his cricket.

On the second-last day of the Test, 'Wok' ran his laps and finished off with exercises which included a routine of pumping his arms up and down in the air. I watched him doing this and decided we could have a bit of fun here.

Our masseur for that match was a black Jamaican named Teddy, who had represented his country as a boxer at the Commonwealth Games. When Johnny had finished his training ritual that evening, I said: " 'Wok', Teddy wasn't too impressed by those Black Power signals you were giving out there on the track and I heard him say he's going to get you and fix you up tonight."

Johnny turned pale and said: "Jeez, I wasn't doing Black Power signals, I was just doing my exercises. What can I do? How can I get out of being fixed up?"

"Well," I said, "Teddy's a very fit guy, but I've noticed he smokes. So if I were you, I'd leave three or four packets of Benson and Hedges and three or four packets of Rothmans for him outside your door before you go to bed tonight. You know, sort of a peace offering. I'll make sure Teddy gets the message in a roundabout way. It'll probably save your skin."

"Gee, thanks mate," he said. "I'll certainly do that."

I was working for Rothmans then and Benson and Hedges were sponsoring the tour, so cigarette supplies were no problem.

Johnny had a few drinks with Terry Jenner, my room-mate, and me that night but left us fairly early to turn in. I gave him half an hour and tip-toed along to his room to see if he'd fallen for my little hoax. Had he ever! There, stacked very neatly outside his door, were four packets of each product.

I picked up an iron chair from the motel patio, banged it around and made the noises I thought an angry black masseur might make as he tried to break down a door. Then I picked up the cigarettes and went back to my room.

About half an hour after Terry and I went to bed, there was a knock on our door. It was Jeff Hammond, Johnny's room-mate.

"What have you done to 'Wok'?" Jeff asked. "I can't get into my room. I've banged on the door and I've shouted through the keyhole, but he won't let me in."

I told him not to worry, to use the extra bed in our room and we'd tell him about it in the morning. Johnny was along to our room bright and early next day and I said: "How did you get on last night, 'Wok'? Did Teddy get you?"

"No, no," said Johnny. "But by God he tried! He took the cigarettes, but he didn't get me!" I think he still believes I saved him from a beating.

We played a lot of cards on tour – on any tour – and we introduced Johnny to a game called Switch. It's a kids' game really, and involves simply following suit, or changing suit, by putting, say a three of clubs on top of a three of diamonds. But when you played 'Wok' you didn't necessarily have to put a three on a three. You could put a six – or anything you liked – on a three and change suit with any other card of your choice at any time you liked.

Johnny would play on regardless, never suspecting he was being taken for a ride. We could have taken him to the cleaners every day – but you didn't do that to a nice, trusting guy like 'Wok' Watkins.

One of the tour games was a four-day match against Trinidad at Point-a-Pierre. I took Johnny aside on the eve of the game and said: "Look, 'Wok', this is one of your last chances on this trip. You're bowling magnificently in the nets, you're dropping it on a threepence every time you send it down.

"All you've got to do when you get out on the field tomorrow is relax and bowl the same way you do in the nets."

'Wok' could relax pretty well, too. On the team bus on the way home from the ground, he'd be the first to lean into a song, and his favourite song was undoubtedly

What Shall We Do With A Drunken Sailor.

With this in mind, I said: "Look, mate, I've got it. What Shall We Do With A Drunken Sailor's your favourite song, right? Right. Okay, what you do as you run in to bowl tomorrow is whistle that song. Don't sing it, just whistle it. I reckon that'll relax you completely and you'll drop the ball on the spot every time."

"Righto," said Johnny, "I'll give anything a try."

I was fielding at mid-on when Johnny was called into the attack next day and as he measured out his run, I said: "Now don't forget what we were talking about last night." He assured me he wouldn't.

So Johnny walked briskly back to his mark, came in whistling – and bowled the widest four wides you ever saw. He damned near hit the square-leg umpire on the way through to the fence.

The other guys were aware of my whistling ploy and had to fight back tears of laughter.

Not to worry, 'Wok', I told him. Perhaps his run-up hadn't been quite right. He measured it out again . . . one, two, three, four, five, six. "You're right," he said. "It was a bit out."

"Give it another go," I insisted, "and don't forget to whistle."

So in he came again, whistling his favourite song – and bowled four wides down the off-side. This one just escaped the out-stretched hand of point as it ran to the boundary.

Two balls, eight runs – and he hadn't got within a bull's roar of the batting surface. The batsman must have wondered if this was a cricket match or a circus.

That was 'Wok' Watkins' only tour. In fact, I don't think he ever bowled again. But he remains one of my most unforgettable characters.

10

A WING, A PRAYER, A SKINFUL

Why should grown men who should know better want to sit in an aeroplane and attempt drinking records as they fly across the world? Beats me. Maybe it's to combat boredom or to forestall jetlag. Maybe it's a spirit of adventure. Maybe it's just thirst.

Whatever it is, or was, my name became linked with these frivolous, liver-defying exploits – and for that I blame Rodney Marsh.

It was Marshie who started it all, on the way home from the West Indies in 1973. As we boarded the plane in Trinidad he asked: "How many beers do you reckon we'll have between here and Sydney?" I said it was a 30-hour flight, so we'd have 25 cans. "You gotta be joking," said 'Bacchus'. "If it's a 30-hour flight, we'll have 35!"

There was no point in arguing, but I reminded him that we'd have to slip in a little sleeping somewhere along the track. And off we went.

We touched down at Bermuda and there we stayed for two-and-a-half hours because of a mechanical problem. Perhaps one of the engines had fallen off, I was never really sure. We didn't leave the plane and the delay went on and on, but they were nice enough to keep serving drinks and by the time we were airborne again, they'd run out of beer.

Marshie, a stickler for detail and fair play, insisted on a change of rules. "What we'll do," he said, "is just make them alcoholic drinks from now on. A bottle of Scotch – the little nip bottle – that'll count as one can of beer. Or a nip bottle of rum, brandy, gin or whatever, that'll count as one can. Then when dinner comes, the half-bottle of wine they serve with meals, that'll be equivalent to a can. Okay?"

It was difficult to dispute that sort of logic and by the time we reached the United States, we were well into the 20s. It looked like being quite a trip. As we approached San Francisco, 'Bacchus' decided to upgrade his target from 35 cans – or substitute spirits or wine – to 40. Being a more conservative soul, I advanced my own goal from 25 to 30. They restocked the plane with beer in 'Frisco and I must say it was nice to taste the old amber again after all the other stuff with which we'd been assaulting the system.

Fatigue started to set in after we left San Francisco. The plane was in darkness and most of the passengers were asleep. Eventually, after a few more beers, Marshie and I decided that was the way we'd go, too. Rodney stretched himself across three vacant seats up the back and he couldn't have had too much faith in the pilot or the plane because he locked himself in with two seatbelts. A bit like wearing braces *and* a belt to keep your pants up. And there he lay, looking much like a beached dugong.

I stumbled back to my seat and had barely shut the eyes when Alan McGilvray tapped me on the shoulder. "I've finally found you," he said. "I've been looking all over the plane for you. You're coming upstairs to have a drink in the first class cabin. And where's that fat little mate of yours? He's coming too!"

We needed a drink like a hole in the head, but what can you do when a lovely bloke like Alan McGilvray seeks you out for a sip? So up we went, neither Marshie nor me in any great shape at all, and we had a few very slow beers.

When the steward came along with refills, I asked him how long we were out of Honolulu and he said about one-and-a-half hours. That suited me fine because I figured at the pace we were going two more beers would occupy that time, and then we could call it a night.

Doesn't time fly when you're having a drink! When next I asked the steward how far we were out of Honolulu, he said three-and-a-half hours. "Hang on," I said, "two hours ago you said we were only one-and-a-half hours out and now you tell me three-and-a-half hours. How can that be?"

"Because we were through Honolulu when you asked the first time," he said. "We're one-and-a-half hours out of Nandi now!" Thank God I wasn't navigator on *that* flight.

We slept from Nandi and, considering the amount and variety we'd consumed, Marshie and I lobbed in Sydney in reasonable condition. I'm not sure how many we'd had, but it must have been 39 or 40 cans, or the equivalent thereof under Rodney's formula.

So that was the trip that started the drinkathons. Every overseas flight after that followed a similar pattern. Bacchus would say well, it's a 22-hour flight to london, so how many do you reckon? It was a bit of a challenge, and he was always the instigator.

I was credited with a record 44 cans on the flight to England in 1977. I didn't actually keep score, but 'Bacchus' insisted it was 44 so that would have to be somewhere around the mark.

There were a few tearaways on that trip – Kim Hughes and some of the other younger guys. The Young Bulls, we called them. They'd tear in and knock a few over. We figured we were the Old Bulls, that we'd take our time and do the lot.

The Young Bulls would start to sink spirits at a furious pace as soon as the wheels left the ground and by the time we reached Singapore they were finding it difficult to scratch. They didn't have another drink all the way to London.

I was out of international cricket by the time the 1983 World Cup came along, so Marshie went it alone. And did he go!

He beat my 44 cans by one – and that last one was downed as the plane taxied into Heathrow Airport in London. I was in the travel business at the time and I took a touring party to England to watch the Cup. Naturally, I ran into Bacchus. I told him I'd seen a film clip of his arrival in London and he didn't look all that flash.   Marshie's recollection of it went like this:

"I wasn't too bad until I got out into the cold air. When I got to the customs desk, they asked me for my passport and I told them it was in my travel bag. And when I bent over to fish it out, I went arse over tit. Over and over.

"The customs bloke eventually came around and emptied my bag, but the passport wasn't there. I actually got into England without a passport – which was found next day on the plane, in the pocket of the seat in front of me.

"I got to the Waldorf Hotel about 10 o'clock in the morning, dropped my bags in the corner of the room and collapsed on top of the bed because I hadn't slept all the way over. And I woke up damn near 24 hours later.

"It took me a while to collect my thoughts, but I

noticed an empty can on top of the fridge so I figured I must have had a nightcap just for practice."

Most of the other guys in that party played golf the day after they arrived, and Marshie was still well and truly sleeping it off when they left for the course. And who should be sitting at the bar – looking immaculate, fresh as a daisy and sipping a big beer – when they arrived back at the Waldorf? R.W. Marsh no less. It fractured them.

I told 'Bacchus' I could not allow him the record because he'd started from Melbourne, not Sydney, and had therefore pinched an hour on me. I also pointed out that he'd had a series of pacemakers all the way from Australia, and that wasn't quite cricket.

Marshie grinned, called me a sore loser and immediately dismissed both protests. I believe his 45-can record has since gone by the board and that the reigning champion is Neil Brooks, the Olympic swimmer. No wonder they call Brooks and his mates The Mean Machine!

There's a saying "like father like son" and my oldest son Brynley followed in Dad's footsteps by setting what is believed to be a drinking record for the flight from Sydney to Perth. Brynley had 15 cans – and he wasn't yet 12 years old!

But before you start shouting "Disgraceful!" and start dialling the child welfare people, let me assure you it was only Coca-Cola!

Brynley was very keen to see my comeback to cricket in the summer of '88 in the one-day games between the 1977 Centenary Test "oldies", so Caroline and I put him on a plane to stay with relatives in Perth until we arrived.

It was quite an adventure for him to fly all that way unchaperoned and when we phoned to make sure he'd

arrived safely, he couldn't wait to tell us about all that Coke he'd had on the way over.

More than anything else, I think he enjoyed sitting back pressing the buzzer for the stewardess, and, having her wait on him like some VIP. The fact that the Coke was free wouldn't have discouraged him either, although he's not a great drinker of the product at home.

On the way from Perth to Adelaide for the second series, Brynley sat next to Dennis Lillee and Rodney Marsh. I'd been telling the boys about my son's claim to the Sydney-Perth record and Dennis, as straight-faced as you like, assured him that the best-ever Coke-drinking performance on a Perth-Adelaide flight was 12 cans. He likes a challenge, does Brynley, and his attempt on this record was immediately set in motion.

Dennis was ordering the cans four at a time and when we touched down in Adelaide, Brynley was just short of the figure which had been plucked out of the air.

I'll never encourage him to drink anything stronger than Coke – but I reckon there's a lot of his dad in young Brynley Walters.

11

THE EMU OF GOVE

If you'd happened to be in the TAB Agency at Gove, in the Northern Territory, on Easter Monday, 1988, you'd have thought, with justification, that Doug Walters had fallen on very hard times. There he was, on all fours, picking up discarded betting tickets.

At the racetracks, they call people like that emus – and the practice is closely associated with having the backside out of your pants.

Things weren't entirely the way they seemed in that betting shop. It was just another pitfall along the impossible road to a punting fortune.

I was in Gove for a speaking engagement during the Calder Shield cricket carnival and, Easter Saturday being one of the major days on the Sydney racing calendar (and me being fond of a bet), I sought out the local TAB to put my money where I thought my horse sense was.

I placed my bets, heard a few race results as I watched the cricket that afternoon, and returned to the TAB to check out the ones I'd missed. It wasn't particularly good news. In fact, I got back only half my outlay but on the way out the door I noticed they were betting that night on the Moonee Valley trots in Melbourne and the Wentworth Park dogs in Sydney.

THE EMU OF GOVE!

What the hell, I thought, why not throw good money after bad and give this lot a fly. I had a bet on every race at either venue, plus doubles and trebles, and walked out with a pocketful of tickets.

I was back on Easter Monday to check the outcome of my punting and as I walked in the woman behind the counter said, "Oh Doug, you'll be wanting this results sheet. You'll find Moonee Valley on the front and Wentworth Park on the back." You certainly couldn't complain about the service.

I stood there checking my tickets against the sheet. Moonee Valley race 1, No. 4. No good. So I threw that ticket on the floor. Race 2, No. 8. Late scratching, so I'd get my money back. I put that ticket aside. Race 3, No. 9. A winner! Paid $4.40. Nice result. I put that ticket aside, too. Race 4, No. 5. No good. Throw that on the floor. Race 5, No. 6. No good. In the bin. Race 6, No. 3. A winner – and it's paid $17.70. You little beauty! Race 7, No. 4. Another winner. Paid $2.20. Race 8, No. 10. No good. On the floor. Race 9, No. 3. A winner. Paid $9.90, thank you very much. Race 10, No. 1. No good. In the bin with that one. Now for the double. Nos. 9 and 3. Got it! You beauty. Dividend of $19.80. How long had this been going on!

I flipped over to the Wentworth Park results and started the procedure all over again. Race 1, no good. On the floor. Race 2, likewise. In the bin. Race 3, a late scratching. Money back. Put that ticket aside. Race 4, a winner. Paid $2.80. Put that aside. Races 5, 6 and 7, no good. On the floor. Race 8, no good. In the bin. Race 9, a winner. Paid 95 cents. Not much of a result, but better than a loser. Race 10, no good. On the floor. Treble and daily double no good. On the floor.

I now had tickets from one end of the TAB to the other, but I did a little quick arithmetic and calculated that I'd turned my $80 outlay into something between $600 and $700. A very nice night's work, I thought, hoping at the same time that they had enough money in the shop to pay me.

My immediate impulse was to cunningly leak the story to the media. I even pictured the headlines: DOUG WALTERS BREAKS BANK AT GOVE... MILLION-DOLLAR DOUG CRIPPLES TAB. Then I thought that would be far too ostentatious so I'd keep it to myself.

I approached the woman behind the counter with a nonchalant air but just a suggestion of a smile. We big winners like to play it cool, you know. I handed her my winning tickets and she started to punch them through the machine.

"Doug," she said, "I'm sorry, but the first one's no good."

"Perhaps I've made a mistake," I said. "Wouldn't be the first time."

I knew something was amiss when she stopped and frowned. "What results sheet did I give you?" she asked. I retrieved the sheet from the other counter and gave it to her. "Oh gawd," she said, "these are last week's results!"

A picture of sixty or seventy $10 notes flying out the TAB window flashed through my mind. Then I summed up the situation. What I had were nine or 10 tickets which were very likely worthless. Around me on the shop floor, and in the bin, among hundreds of other tickets, were 20-odd of mine which may not be worthless.

The woman was very apologetic. "It's my fault," she said, "and I'll help you find your tickets." There had been heavy traffic through the TAB all day and you can imagine the number of discarded tickets. The floor was damned near carpeted with them and the bins damned near overflowing.

It was acutely embarrassing down there on the floor, crawling between the legs of bemused customers. My face is not exactly unknown around Australia and I'm sure just about everyone in there knew who I was. They were nice enough to refrain from the obvious comments. You know: "Lost your contact lenses, Doug?" Or: "If you're going *that* bad, Doug, I'll lend you a couple of bucks."

Meanwhile, the woman was rummaging through the bins. "Moonee Valley race 4... is that one of yours, Doug?" she'd ask. "Moonee Valley race 4? Yes, that'd be one of mine." And so it went on.

We managed to find most of my tickets and when she put them through the machine, it gave me a result of $17. A paltry return on an $80 outlay and not even worth the embarrassment of being an emu.

So I hadn't quite broken the bank after all. But I sure gave the Gove TAB customers something to talk about.

Cricketers, on the whole, like a bet on the horses as much as anyone, and perhaps more than most. Kerry O'Keeffe went a step further and actually bought himself a hayburner, or an interest in one, during the World Series Cricket days.

See what happens when you've played cricket for peanuts for years and suddenly find yourself in the money. A man can become a spendthrift!

We were playing a game in Rockhampton and Kerry took us into his confidence on the team bus on the way to the ground.

"I've got this horse having his first start today," he said. The name's Vivatus and he's running at Canterbury. Anyone want to have a bet?"

Do tell us more, we begged.

"Well," said Kerry, "Vivatus is bred along staying lines, but we're starting him out over 1000 metres. Anyone want to have a bet?" A huge joke, we thought, expecting anyone to back a stayer racing first-up over 1000, and we told Kerry so. "Suit yourself," he said, "but don't come crying to me when he bolts in at 100/1."

We listened to Vivatus' debut that afternoon and it's fair to say he didn't exactly set the racing world on fire. The racecaller mentioned him just twice in running each time to say: "... and Vivatus a distant last".

We kept listening, and the caller had gone through the breeding and ownership of the placegetters and the should-pays before Vivatus crossed the line.

I'm afraid we gave Kerry a bad time, and I laughed louder and longer than most. "Right," he said, "I'll never tell you anything about horses again and I certainly won't tell you when Vivatus is going to win."

And neither he did. A damn shame really because Vivatus went on to win four races – three of them in the city. And, to make things worse, in each of those city starts Vivatus was at more than 100/1!

12

TIME ON OUR HANDS

Like him or not, you had to have great respect for Ian Botham's cricketing ability. You wonder just how good he might have been had adverse publicity not dogged him like a bailiff.

I'm not suggesting Botham didn't earn his notoriety and you can't really blame the media for cashing in on it. A more discreet personality inside the Botham body might have amounted to an even better cricketer. Then again, take away the fire and the result may have been just another player.

We'll never know now and there's no way I'm going to sit in judgement on the guy. I bring his name up here simply because he still owes me a few quid.

I met Ian Botham during the 1975 tour of England. He was playing for Somerset and had not yet made his Test debut. I was third selector on that tour and took over the captaincy for the match against Somerset when Ian and Greg Chappell decided to sit it out.

Kerry O'Keeffe was playing for the county at that stage and at the end of the first day's play he mentioned that Botham sold watches for a living when he wasn't playing cricket and maybe our blokes would like to see them. You know, lasting souvenirs of the tour, presents to take home, that sort of thing.

"Sure," I said, "send him along. I'll probably buy some myself. I'm not much of a shopper and I'll need something to take home for presents."

TIME ON OUR HANDS ...!

So Botham fronted in the Australian dressing room with a tray full of his wares. They were digital watches, quite new on the market, quite a novelty.

"How much?" I asked.

"Thirteen pounds 50 pence," said Botham. Seemed pretty reasonable to me, so I took half a dozen. No shopping for me, and I'd be No. 1 on the popularity parade when I handed them out back home.

The other guys had the same idea and I reckon Botham sold six dozen of his watches among the team. He departed obviously well pleased with his salesmanship and there were no complaints from us. No complaints, that is, until I had a casual chat with David Lloyd during our next match.

David, who played for Lancashire and had represented England a few times, asked how I'd enjoyed Somerset, how did I like 'that chap Botham' and had he sold me any watches.

Somerset? Fine, had a pretty good time? Botham? He was all right. And watches?

"Funny you should ask that," I said. "As a matter of fact, I bought half a dozen. He must have sold about six dozen between the team."

The price? Thirteen pounds 50, I said.

"You know you can buy them for eleven pounds 50 at any store around here," said David.

I walked down the street the following day and, sure enough, the same watches were retailing at eleven pounds 50. We'd been done, neatly and nicely.

Next time I see Botham I'll remind him he owes me 12 quid. I won't haggle over inflation, exchange rates or anything like that. I'll just accept the dozen.

In the meantime, I'll follow some old advice and never trust anyone who sells watches.

13

MAKING A SPLASH

You meet all sorts of characters in the course of a cricketing career – some memorable, some you'd prefer to forget in a hurry. I'll never forget a bloke I met at Port Macquarie, NSW, in 1984 – and I still don't even know his name. No doubt we'll be having a chat if our paths cross again.

I was in Port Macquarie for a game sponsored by Tooheys, and, when it was over I was having a beer with Steve Rixon and a guy I assumed to be a mate of his. We were standing at the bar, shouting in turn and having a chat. I wondered why Steve hadn't bothered to introduce me to his mate, but what the hell, he seemed a decent enough sort of guy, a pleasant enough drinking companion. And what's in a name anyhow?

It went on for some time and when they eventually closed the bar we decided to grab a couple of beers out of our rooms and continue our little session beside the hotel pool. Port Macquarie's climate is just made for the pursuit of such pleasure.

So I grabbed a couple of Tooheys from my fridge, Steve grabbed a couple of Tooheys from his and his mate grabbed a couple of Foster's from his. Foster's? That didn't seem to be the right sort of beer for after the match we'd just played, but maybe the guy had run out of

... CIGARETTE IN MOUTH, FULL GLASS OF BEER IN HAND !

Tooheys and had tapped into an emergency supply of the 'foreign' stuff. It didn't seem worthy of question or comment.

We were sitting there, legs dangling in the pool, drinking this beer and generally reflecting on life when Steve's mate got to his feet, sneaked around behind – and pushed me in!

Under I went, cigarette in mouth, full glass of beer in hand. I came up spluttering and intent on revenge, but Steve's mate had dived in at the other end, climbed out the other side and bolted.

I told Steve I suddenly didn't particularly care for his choice of mates and he said: "*My* mate? I've never seen him before in my life! I thought he was *your* mate!"

So there we'd been, drinking all night with a total stranger. The clown's probably still dining out on the story of how he pushed Doug Walters into a swimming pool in Port Macquarie.

I asked around next morning and all I could find out was that he came from Canberra. Which probably explains his irrational behaviour.

14

BEWARE THE BOMBAY BIRDIE

G ive an Australian cricketer a day off on tour and chances are he'll head for the golf course. The two sports are quite compatible, each calling for a high degree of rhythm and timing – although it pays to eliminate the square-cut and the hook from your tee shots.

Cricket has produced some damned good golfers over the years. Random examples are Bob Simpson, Ted Dexter and Richie Benaud, who still play off a low mark. And while Rodney Marsh will never beat brother Graham, you or I wouldn't want to play him for too many dollars.

I played a lot of golf on a lot of foreign courses. Some of my scores were mediocre, others would have done justice to Bradman at the crease. For sheer comedy there was nothing to compare with the 17th hole at 'Royal Bombay' during the 1969 tour of India.

You could never compare 'Royal Bombay' with, say, Royal Melbourne. The scarcity of water is always a problem in India; in fact, if it doesn't rain, a course gets no water at all.

So the fairways are rock hard, which gives you a lot of bounce and a lot of run. Unfortunately, they are also quite uneven and your ball is likely at any time to take a huge bounce sideways into what the locals would call rough, but we would call jungle.

The 17th at 'Royal Bombay' was particularly challenging because it was a long par five and the tee was set back in the jungle, with a lot of long grass to negotiate before you hit the fairway.

Ian Chappell, Brian Taber and a 'Royal Bombay' member made up our four that day and we had the mandatory two caddies each – one to carry your bag, the other to chase your ball up the fairway or into the rough and put a small, upturned jam tin over it.

I'd inquired politely about the tin on the first hole and was told it was to protect the ball from marauding crows. Even at that stage it looked like being a most interesting round of golf.

I'm not a great user of a wood on a golf course, but the 17th being a par five, I pulled out the driver and was taking practice swings as Brian addressed his ball. On my third swing, the club slipped from my sweaty, ungloved hand and sailed away into the dense jungle behind the tee.

As the club came to rest in a treetop 60 feet above the ground, 'Chappelli' stifled laughter and said, mock-seriously: "For Christ's sake, 'Freddie', are you here to play golf, or are you just going to stuff around?"

My caddy (the bag-carrying one) was unfazed by it all. He ran off into the jungle and started climbing the tree in pursuit of my flyaway wood. "Don't worry, mate," I shouted, "I'll buy a new club. Come back."

I'd borrowed my set from the club and was quite happy to make good the loss. I had visions of the little bloke being snapped up by a tiger, or emerging from the jungle wearing a king cobra. And I didn't want that sort of thing on my conscience.

"Not to concern yourself, sahib," he shouted back. "I find. I fix."

So the little guy continued to climb the tree and while all this was going on, Brian Taber had regained his composure and teed off. He duffed the shot into the long grass, but so hard was the ground underneath that the ball kept bouncing. It disappeared into the grass 20 or 30 times but kept bobbing up again in all directions. Talk about trick shots!

His ball eventually came to rest on the only bare patch of ground within coo-ee of the ladies' tee about 40 yards away. By this time, the caddy had returned with my errant club. I teed off and we strode away to inflict further punishment on our respective balls.

Alas, Brian's caddy (the tin-toting one) was not quite quick enough this time. A crow beat him to the ball by a couple of yards, picked it up, flew into the jungle and was never seen again.

I immediately declared it a lost ball and penalised Brian the regulation two strokes.

If you're looking for a different round of golf, I strongly recommend 'Royal Bombay.' But watch that par five 17th: there are hazards you wouldn't believe.

A CROW BEAT HIM TO THE BALL ...!

15

BONE LAZY

When we were preparing for Kerry Packer's World
Series Cricket revolution, it was made quite clear
to us that professionalism was going to be the name of
the game – and in more ways than one. We were being
paid like professionals and Packer obviously expected us
to play accordingly. Which led to the consideration of
physical fitness.

There was no doubt that the WSC hierarchy's
interpretation of fitness was going to mean longer and
harder training sessions than would appeal to Doug
Walters. I was never one for the iron-man physical stuff.
I regarded batting as largely a matter of eye and timing
and I couldn't see prolonged sessions of self-torture
doing much for those faculties.

Someone once told me when I was a kid back in
Dungog that you would save yourself a lot of
unnecessary running if you gave ones, twos and threes
a bit of a miss and made the boundary your objective as
often as possible. I could see the need for specialist fast
bowlers putting the miles into their legs on the track but,
as we all know, they're a race apart.

By the time Australia toured New Zealand in 1977,
most of us were already in the WSC outfield. It was still
all very hush-hush and some of the guys – including

yours truly – were actually recruited on that tour. Greg Chappell was captain and, in line with the WSC edict that physical fitness was to be a commitment, he pulled an early-morning training run on our first full day in Christchurch.

It had been a pretty full night, actually. Rod Marsh and I had seen out the last over in the bar of our hotel and a 6 a.m. gallop around Christchurch was just what I didn't need next day.

By the time I arrived down in the foyer in my running shorts, the other guys were jogging out the door. I jogged along a respectable 400-500 yards behind. If questioned, I'd have said I was saving my sprint for the run home.

The route Greg had mapped out took us across a bridge over the Avon River, but the old Walters' cunning prevailed, and, I managed to save myself quite a bit of ground by taking another bridge a little upstream before tagging on to the main bunch. Questioned, I'd have said I became momentarily lost.

So far, so good – and there was better to come, in the shape of a cemetery. Now, everyone knows a cemetery is the ultimate resting place, and I was already in need of rest. So as the other blokes ran on along the torture trail, I did a couple of neat sidesteps at the rear and ducked down behind a headstone.

No worries here, I thought, I'd wait for the main body (if you'll pardon the term) to retrace its steps in five or 10 minutes, tack on to the rear again and arrive back at the hotel puffing and blowing with the very best, and, most conscientious of them.

I'd figured without the severity of the fitness campaign and was still hiding out more than an hour later.

There is little to do, I found, when you're a fugitive from your brothers in a foreign cemetery. You can, after

BONE LAZY!

all, memorise only so many headstone inscriptions; and you don't want to mentally dwell on death at any particular stage of life.

I was seriously thinking of walking (and I emphasise *walking*) back to the hotel and throwing myself on the mercy of Greg Chappell. It was a pretty grim prospect, but more appealing at that stage than sitting on a perfectly strange grave which, if you'll again pardon the irreverence, is dead boring.

I broke cover just in time to see, in the distance, the boys returning from their marathon and dived behind a headstone just in time to escape detection. What a weary, bedraggled bunch they were. You'd have sworn they'd just run the length of the South Island.

Doug Walters, all rested up and as fresh as a daisy, tacked on unnoticed behind and called on previously-untapped acting skills to be puffing like a 19th Century locomotive when we made it back to the hotel. I may be the only Australian Test cricketer to have spent a training session in a New Zealand graveyard.

The physical fitness thing became very much a part of the WSC scene. I can see better now why the Packer people wanted to present their players in top shape to a super-curious public. This was the ultimate challenge to the cricket Establishment and it had to be made to work.

The image we presented on the field was going to be all-important. We had to look like finely-tuned athletes and play accordingly.

Among the fitness requirements was what we called the quarter-hour torture test, this involved running 3400 metres in 15 minutes. When you look at it, that's two miles and a couple of hundred yards-plus in the old language; in other words, a long long way – and there weren't too many Emil Zatopeks among us.

Still, most of the guys made it through. Even I beat the pain barrier and qualified. The stragglers were Martin Kent and Gary Gilmour and it reached the stage, with an important match coming up in Perth, when an ultimatum was delivered: shape up or cop a $1000 fine each.

That did the trick for Martin, who must have had dollar signs flashing before his eyes at the next test, which he passed. It left 'Gus' looking down the barrel on his own. Gary was never one of your fleet-footed iron men. Grant Kenny would have felt safe in his company. But rules were rules. He was on his last chance.

I thought it pretty ironical that Ian Chappell should ask me – one of the less physically-inclined members of the squad – to supervise Gary's big test. Maybe there was a cryptic message in there somewhere.

Anyway, the venue for Gary's trial-by-ordeal was to be the Gloucester Park trotting track, which WSC had made its Perth headquarters after being frozen out of the WACA Ground directly opposite.

Gloucester Park was, and probably still is, the best harness racing venue in Australia and it turned out to be a more-than-reasonable cricket arena, too, considering it was converted almost overnight.

I got Gary organised on the track, set my watch and told him I'd yell "stop" when his 15 minutes were up. And off he went like a two-legged Village Kid. On the stroke of 15 minutes later, he pulled up looking like last man home in a Death Valley marathon.

"Well, how did I go? Did I make it?" he asked between gasps, pants and wheezes. "Gee, I don't know," I replied. "How the hell are we going to measure it? I hadn't thought about that."

"Oh Christ," said 'Gus'. "*Now* you tell me! Look, I've got a thousand bucks riding on this. I gotta know!"

He suggested I retrace his steps and count the paces. Then we'd measure my stride, get hold of a pocket calculator, do a couple of sums and come up with an answer which hopefully would be 3400 metres, or, something in excess.

I told him he was out of his mind. No way was Doug Walters going to run around a trotting track in the dark (which it was by now).

Sometimes (not often, just sometimes) my initiative astounds me. What we'd do, I said, was go back to the hotel, grab one of the team cars, come back to the ground and measure his run on the speedo. 'Gus' was a desperate man by this stage and would have tried anything. We fetched a car, drove out on to the track (and I'm not sure the WA Trotting Association would have approved) and began the pursuit of Gary Gilmour's moment of truth.

Bingo! At journey's end, the speedo clock said he'd filled his metres quota with a few to spare.

As we drove back to our hotel, 'Gus' couldn't find words to adequately describe his feelings towards me. "You're a real mate, Doug," he said (among other nice things). "I owe you for this and if there's ever anything I can do to repay you, just say the word."

Did he really mean that? "Sure," he said, "bet your life I do."

"Okay," I said, "let's go for a run around the park to build up a thirst. Then you can spend a bit of that thousand bucks I just saved you on a few beers."

We gave the run around the park a miss, but Gary bought very well, and very often, that night.

16

HEAVY GOING AT THE HILL

Sportsmen's nights can be a lot of fun – and the comedy is not always strictly according to the script. They can lead a bloke into some pretty bizarre situations, as I found on a trip to Broken Hill in 1983 to speak at an Australian Rules football function.

I had a premonition that this was going to be no ordinary assignment when my flight touched down at The Hill at 7.30 a.m. and there was no-one to meet me as arranged. Then I realised they go on Adelaide time up there, so no wonder. Still, you're a long way from nowhere to be met by no-one.

The plane had already turned around and taken off back to Sydney when some local guy at the airport recognised me and asked who was supposed to be meeting me. I told him and he said: "Oh, he works down the mines, but I know where he lives. Jump in the car and we'll go around to his place." Which we did, only to be told by the maid that yes, he was at work down the mines.

We were getting nowhere fast, but we eventually ran the bloke to earth at the mine and he promptly gave me a conducted tour of the Broken Hill underground.

Next stop was the pub and the first glasses were raised at 11.45 a.m., which was probably a little too early

I LEARNED VERY QUICKLY THAT DRINKING IS THE No. 1 PASTIME AT BROKEN HILL!

because I had to address the football dinner that night.

I learned very quickly that drinking is the No. 1. pastime in Broken Hill. There is, after all, very little else to do. So we settled in to a long, lively session and I was feeling no pain at all when we arrived at the footy club at 8 p.m.

The place was packed – about 500 people, I'd reckon – and the news came through that the flight carrying Max Walker, who was to be co-speaker, was running late. So I went on first, did my bit and was about to wind up with a ripper of a punchline when someone whispered that Maxie was running even later and could I go on for a bit longer.

Max eventually arrived about 9.45 p.m. and just as he was starting his monologue, an almighty electrical storm broke. Thunder, lightning, torrential rain – the lot. The lights went out, the power went off and there was a scream from the bar. The barman had fallen through a glass partition. They told us later he'd been struck by lightning, but I didn't know that could happen indoors. Maybe it zapped him through an open window.

The crowd, well oiled by this stage, regarded the blackout as a huge joke and it wasn't until someone started screaming for doctors, nurses and ambulances that order was restored and the barman was despatched to hospital.

The emergency lighting was on by now, but we were still without other power. We were off the air for half an hour and just as Max finished his spiel, in walked the barman, bandaged up like Rick McCosker in his second innings of the Centenary Test. There was blood all over his clothing, but they are pretty tough customers at The Hill, and he got straight back behind the bar and started pouring beers.

The beer had warmed right up during the power failure and Maxie and I decided rum would be our go. So we sat there downing Bundy and Coke until 4 a.m. – and me having to catch a 7 a.m. (6.30 in Broken Hill language) flight back to Adelaide! And wait there four hours for a Sydney connection.

I had the sunglasses on and the head down when I reached Adelaide airport – and who did I bump into but Dennis Lillee and Rod Marsh, who had just played a Sheffield Shield match against South Australia and were on their way back to Perth.

'Bacchus', being a very hospitable man, immediately asked me upstairs for a beer. The suggestion, after the day and night I'd just had, sent a minor shudder through me but he insisted and I said okay, I'd just have one of those very little beers.

The first sip tasted awful but someone up there must have loved me, because they gave the boarding call for the Perth flight and Rodney and Dennis had to down their drinks and go.

It was one of the few times I've left half a glass of beer on a bar, but who needed it! I found a nice deep chair in the passenger lounge downstairs and slept for three hours until my flight to Sydney.

I'd left my car at Sydney airport and as I slid behind the wheel I was thinking that Broken Hill was a fun place but they sure knew how to serve up a hangover there. Which made me wonder if I should be at the wheel at all.

Drink-driving was a very hot topic in NSW at the time. Random breath-testing had just been introduced and the message was certainly getting through.

I sat there for a couple of minutes and did a bit of a countback. No, I'd be right. It was getting on for 5 p.m. and I'd had only half a glass of beer in the past 13 hours. No worries. Home we go, Doug.

It was 4.55 p.m. when I was pulled up by a breath-testing unit on the other side of the Gladesville Bridge. I was second in line, behind a motorbike, which gave me just enough time to panic!

Hang on, what did that anti-drink-drive commercial say? Three middies will make you .05 and you can only have the equivalent of one every hour or lose the equivalent of one every hour after you stop drinking.

Christ, where did that put me? I'd drunk from 11.45 a.m. to 4 a.m. and that included a goodly go at rum. Even if I'd averaged only three drinks an hour, by their calculations I'd be over the limit for two days!

91

Fortunately, I'd done tests on myself at the Brewery and found out that it left my system much quicker, but not being tested that day, one never knows.

I went hot and cold as I imagined the consequences. A court appearance, the worst sort of publicity, and a long-lasting stigma which your family would have to share.

The mind and stomach were turning over apace when the policeman approached and asked me to blow into the bag, which I did. "No, no," he said, "keep on blowing until I tell you to stop." So I gave it the full burst and he said whoa, that would do.

Then he studied the thing and said: "That's a negative reading. You may proceed. Sorry for the inconvenience."

Negative reading? Mechanical failure, I'd say!

I wasn't about to question the reading and demand another go. I smiled politely, said thank you – and was still trembling when I drove into the garage at home.

How lucky had I been? Very. And the point was well taken.

You don't have to be clever to know that drinking and driving are a potentially lethal cocktail. But why wait for a close encounter with the law to bring you to your senses?

One of those was one too many for Doug Walters.

And as for sportsmen's nights at Broken Hill? Highly recommended – if you can hack the pace.

17

A WAY WITH WORDS

I've always regarded bullshit as a bit of an art form. There are those who can do it with subtlety and brilliance. There are those far too heavy-handed and obvious to make a go of it. Then there are Wesley Hall and Freddie Trueman.

Talk about the odd couple ... a black West Indian and a white Yorkshireman. They had two things in common: they were great fast bowlers and very, very funny men. When they got together over several drinks in a mutual admiration situation, the dialogue was incredible.

Ian Chappell and I were privy to such an occasion when we took part in a double-wicket competition, part of the Garfield Sobers' benefit in the West Indies in 1975, on our way to the World Cup series in England. The conversation went like this:

Fred: Wes, I wish I could have bowled at your pace. The only thing I would have loved to do is bowl at your pace. Jesus, you were (expletive deleted) quick!

Wes: Oh man, you used to move the ball so (expletive deleted) well, Freddie ... inswingers, outswingers, cut it off the seam, this way and that way. Plus you were pretty quick as well, man.

Fred: Yeah but Wes... boy, you know, if I could have bowled at your pace, that would really have topped it off for me.

Wes: Look Freddie, every ball you bowled was doin' something, through the air or off the wicket. And you weren't slow, man. Every ball you bowled was doin' something.

Fred: Yeah Wes, you're quite right. Looking back on it, you know, every ball I ever bowled did something... swung or jagged back this way or that. Every ball I ever bowled, bar one.

Wes: Freddie, you were a pretty good bowler, but are you telling me every ball you *ever* bowled, bar one? Man, you gotta be havin' me on!

Fred: Aye, come to think of it, even that one bastard might have done a bit!

'Chappelli' and I had heard quite enough. Next thing, Freddie was going to say Wes was the best batsman he'd even seen and it was going to take a small bulldozer to cut a path through the bullshit. We retreated.

Fred Trueman was one of cricket's lovable characters, rough-hewn but a credit to his country. If he did anything better than bowl quick, it was swear. I don't know what religion he is, or if he has a religion at all, but if he were Catholic his typical confession would be along these lines:

"Good evening, Father. I'm sorry, but I said (expletive deleted) yesterday and the (expletive deleted) day before that and some (expletive deleted) annoyed me so I told him to (expletive deleted) off and I'm really (expletive deleted) sorry about that."

Freddie couldn't help the four-letter words and there was something about the way he said them that

somehow made them acceptable. Four little old ladies will back me up on that.

Fred was holding court at the WACA Ground one afternoon during the international double-wicket competition in the late sixties. Bill Lawry was my partner in that event and we were sitting with Fred and some other guys in the front row of the balcony of the old dressing rooms. The four little old ladies were sitting directly below and were obviously hearing every word being said. And there were plenty of words, I can tell you. Freddie was dominating the conversation and four-letter words were dominating his vocabulary.

Maybe he didn't know the ladies were there; maybe he did. Maybe he'd decided they were old enough to have heard those words before. In any event, he held the floor for a good 45 minutes without a suggestion of a complaint from below.

Then one of the other guys in Fred's captive audience made a bad mistake. Reacting to an incident on the field, he jumped to his feet and said: "Oh shit, wouldn't that (expletive deleted) you!"

Shock horror outrage from downstairs. "Excuse me, would you mind your language," snapped one of the little old ladies.

Such was the raw, rustic charm of Freddie Trueman. What he'd been saying for the best part of an hour had suddenly, from another mouth, become highly offensive.

It takes a special personality to get away with that sort of stuff – and Freddie Trueman was a special kind of guy.

18

WHEN JOHNNY RAISED A RIOT

Fast bowlers are traditionally the standover men of cricket. They come boring in, nostrils flared and teeth bared to the breeze, all bully and bluster, all "lookout-you-bastard-I'm-going-to-knock-your-bloody-head-off" And so it should be. Quicks generate most of the excitement in the game and if they didn't have the killer instinct they shouldn't be out there anyway.

Strange, then, that mild-mannered NSW spinner Johnny Gleeson should have been the one to bring on a storm in India in 1969. Stranger still that he should have done it with a bat.

The last game of that tour was in Bangalore and we were in a bit of trouble. Make that a *lot* of trouble. There are degrees of trouble, and 8/36 rates pretty high on the dire scale. It was even worse when you consider that it was our second innings, we were behind on the first innings and there was a full session to go.

The eight of us who had fallen had been fired out leg-before by the Indian umpires who, on the whole, have never been averse to giving those decisions against visiting batsmen. Every time Indian off-spinner Prasanna struck a pad on a wicket that was spinning like a top, up would go the finger and out we'd go. He had 7/11 at that stage.

But all was not lost. We still had two things going for us: Bill Lawry, who'd carried his bat so far for four runs, and the incoming Johnny Gleeson. Johnny was nice and angry, probably because every leg-before appeal he'd shouted in the Indian innings had been turned down.

I'm not saying they cheat in India. Maybe they just bend the rules a little. I never saw an Indian umpire, in a Test situation, give an Australian batsman the benefit of the doubt. But enough of that – we don't want to start an international incident, do we?

Johnny was prepared to . . . and did!

He walked out there waving his bat, windmill fashion, as real batsmen do to loosen up. He stopped at the bowler's end and started waving it, helicopter fashion, around the umpire's head.

We had no way of knowing that Johnny was saying: "Look, you little bastard, if you give me out leg-before wicket, I'm going to wrap this right around your bloody neck. And if you or your mate give Bill Lawry – that bloke at the other end – if you or your mate give him out lbw, then I'll wrap it around the neck of the bloke who gives him out!"

For the next hour and 50 minutes, Johnny and Bill merely padded the ball away. Bill would poke his right pad down the wicket, Johnny his left. There were lots of appeals from an Indian field long accustomed to a raised finger being just a formality. And every time, Johnny would give the umpire the mean eye, raise his bat a little and slip him a wink and a smile when the response was negative.

In the meantime, Bill moved on from four runs to six and the Australian score from 8/36 to 8/39 – the other run being a leg-bye.

HE STOPPED AT THE BOWLER'S END AND
STARTED WAVING IT, HELICOPTER FASHION,
AROUND THE UMPIRE'S HEAD ...!

You could sense impatience and unrest in the crowd long before the rocks, Coke bottles and what-have-you started to rain on to the field with 10 minutes to go. Johnny withdrew his pad from halfway down the wicket, walked briskly over to the square-leg umpire – and declared a State of Emergency!

"Riot," he said. "No more play. We're going home!"

We did. And as our bus driver dodged the missiles on the way out of the ground, we unanimously voted Johnny Gleeson Man of the Match.

"RIOT! NO MORE PLAY – WE'RE GOING HOME!"

19

CLOAK-AND-DAGGER CRICKET

I doubt if the CIA itself could have improved on the secrecy which surrounded the signings of players, here, and everywhere, for Kerry Packer's World Series Cricket. It was a real cloak-and-dagger stuff, and necessarily so. When you consider what was at stake, the timing had to be spot-on.

The Australian team was in Auckland playing New Zealand in a Test at Eden Park in February, 1977 when the Packer people put the hard word on me in circumstances you might describe as bizarre. I hadn't an inkling of what was going on behind the scenes but a few blokes, including Dennis Lillee, were well aware that the World Series time-bomb had been set.

Dennis and Austin Robertson approached me that day at Eden Park and said John Cornell wanted to see me. I knew John very casually and I'd seen him around the team hotel in Auckland, but for all I knew he was simply an Australian cricket fan who'd come over for the Tests.

My appointment with John, I was told, was to be in a vacant dressing room beneath the grandstand. I found the room and couldn't help thinking it would be a good place for a murder. It was stark and bare and lit by a single, naked globe.

I DOUBT IF THE CIA COULD HAVE IMPROVED ON THE SECRECY WHICH SURROUNDED THE SIGNING OF PLAYERS ... !

John and Austin were there when I arrived. Why all this undercover business? If they wanted to see me, why not the hotel or the real dressing room? Maybe they wanted my autograph and were too embarrassed to ask elsewhere.

John made the first move. "Look, Doug," he said, "I'm going a bit bad. Could you lend me a quid?"

"Christ," I thought, "this bastard's got me all the way down here to bite me for a couple of bucks."

John Cornell was, and is, a very dapper guy, a very sharp dresser, and he didn't look to me as if he was going bad at all. But instinctively, I reached for my wallet.

Then he got serious. Would I like to be part of the most exciting development international cricket had ever seen?

Would I what! Would I accept a certain number of dollars – more dollars than I could expect to earn in a career with the Establishment to play a season with and against the best cricketers in the world?

Would I ever! There was no haggling and, really, very little discussion. I was sold. Count me in, I said. We shook hands and parted. Come to think of it, I never did lend John that quid. And from what I hear, he certainly doesn't need it now.

The arrangement with me, and the other WSC recruits, was that one-third of the first season's fee was to be paid up front, a sort of deposit. And again, it was like something out of a spy movie.

My cheque arrived in the MCG dressing room immediately after the Centenary Test which followed the New Zealand series. We'd beaten England in one of the great games of cricket and the atmosphere was unbelievable.

Austin Robertson walked into the room, came up to me and handed me an envelope. "Here are the theatre tickets I promised you," he said.

I could have gone to a lot of theatres on what was inside. Kerry Packer had just made a down payment on Doug Walters' services.

It is one of the great misconceptions of the WSC recruiting blitz that Dennis Lillee was among the first to sign. He was, in fact, the last. He had been deeply involved from the outset and was one of those responsible for the World Series concept itself. His signature was simply overlooked in the frantic pursuit of starters. The omission was discovered – and immediately put right – when heads were being re-counted.

A lot of stories emerged later about the WSC negotiations and signings. Reactions varied a great deal.

There was the direct approach, exemplified by Eddie Barlow, the South African pig farmer and all-rounder. Eddie banged on Austin's door at the Churchill Hotel in London, thrust a beefy paw into Austin's hand and said: "Now where's that contract you want me to sign?"

There was the drawn-out drama of Western Australian batsman Ross Edwards, who had protracted negotiations and even queried Kerry Packer's capacity to pay for it all. "Look," said Austin, after the umpteenth exasperating meeting, "are you going to sign this bloody thing or not?"

"Of course," said Ross. And immediately did.

There was the strange attitude of West Indies paceman Andy Roberts, who had assembled with Clive Lloyd and Viv Richards in a room at the Trinidad Hilton. "I'm going to sign," said Clive. He signed. Viv rolled his eyes and did likewise.

"I'll sign tomorrow," said Andy – and no amount of coercion was going to hurry him up. Maybe he didn't believe in doing today what you could put off till tomorrow. Or maybe his horoscope wasn't favourable that day.

And there was the "ooh, yes please" response of NSW leg-spinner Kerry 'Skull' O'Keeffe. Kerry wasn't doing much at the time!

20

A BUM RAP

Being still on active service, Dennis Lillee had more to prove than most of us in the Centenary Test Revisited Challenge one-day series between Australia and England in 1988. A lot of people had criticised his decision to emerge from retirement and play Sheffield Shield cricket for Tasmania; they regarded it as a self inflicted dent on his image as perhaps the greatest fast bowler the world has seen.

Me? I steer clear of debates like that, mainly because I consider it none of my business. If a guy feels fit enough and motivated enough to give a comeback a fly, then what the hell?

Apart from Dennis, likeable Pom Derek Randall (who still plays County cricket) and David Hookes (who will probably captain South Australia until he qualifies for the age pension), the rest of us were taken out of mothballs for the Challenge series and, if you could ignore the discomfort of using muscles which had lain dormant for years, it was enormous fun.

Things were not looking too good for Dennis in the series opener before his adoring home crowd in Perth. He was probably trying too hard to answer his critics and his line and length were not quite what we had known in the glory years.

At one stage, he looked like going wicketless, but late in the England innings got one through his old enemy Keith Fletcher and sent the stumps flying. Then he wrapped up affairs by giving Derek Underwood the same treatment.

Dennis' figures were 2/31 from 10 overs and as we left the field, Gary (Gus) Gilmour put an arm around his shoulder and said: "Nice going, Sorbent!"

"Sorbent? Whaddayabloodymean Sorbent?" growled Dennis.

"You cleaned up the tail," said 'Gus', at great pains to keep a straight face.

When you're a callow kid at good old Dungog, your interpretation of 'the social whirl' is a ride on the merry-go-round with the girl next door. When you're thrust into international cricket and all its trappings, you learn very quickly about other lifestyles.

Don't get me wrong, whatever you do. I like to think that the Dungog in me prevails. I still think champagne should be drunk out of beer glasses and that there should be a law against eating fish-and-chips any other way than through the hole you've poked in the newspaper wrapping. But you can't be an Australian cricketer touring other countries without being impressed by the lavishness and diversity of the hospitality.

I've taken tea with the Queen at Buckingham Palace; I've been feted by Indian rajahs; I've sipped rum with the cream of Caribbean society (and without crooking the little finger of the drinking hand, I might add). For sheer hospitality, though, I must single out a guy named Des

Derepas, who damned near killed a lot of us with kindness in Brisbane in 1988.

Des is a very senior executive with FAI Insurance, major sponsor of the Centenary Test Revisited series. I knew he was going to be a very formidable host when we were having a drink with him in a tavern bar in the plaza of the Brisbane Hilton. He wouldn't let us buy a beer and the school – a mixture of Aussies and Poms – was growing by the minute.

There were nine or 10 of us there when he decided there had to be a better way. Ferrying beers across from the bar on trays was a little less than sophisticated.

"What we'll do," he said, "is move upstairs into a Hilton bar. I'll open an account there and you chaps can make your own pace. Just chalk it up to FAI and, above all, enjoy yourselves."

Gee, I thought, the Dungog pub was never like this.

We found a plush Hilton bar and spent a painless two or three hours there on the generosity of FAI before Des suggested it might be time for dinner. There was a consensus of consent and Des said: "Leave this entirely to me. I'll make a phone call. Back in a minute."

That was the only fault I could find in Des's performance. He said one minute and it actually took him three. When he got back, he said he'd booked us into the finest seafood restaurant in Brisbane and there'd be cars outside in 10 minutes.

"Which leaves us time for another beer."

Another beer later we walked outside to what the uninitiated might have mistaken for the Brisbane Motor Show. Leading the parked procession was the longest stretch limousine I'd ever seen. A Lincoln. Behind that was a Rolls and bringing up the rear were two Mercedes.

There were eight of us for dinner and four super-luxury cars. Obviously, we all wanted to ride in that long, long Lincoln, but reason won out and the guys figured they had better make use, seeing they were there, of the four cars provided. There were not enough bums to fill seats, so the second Merc was sent home.

I'd been sneaky enough to get a seat in the Lincoln and, really, until you've seen one of these machines, you can only guess. It had three phones, a colour TV set and a bar. While a couple of the other guys were trying to phone the world, I tested the bar. It worked.

Des had said the finest seafood restaurant in Brisbane and he wasn't exaggerating. The food was sensational... mudcrabs, oysters, crayfish, barramundi, prawns. Name a delicacy of the deep and this place had it. Quite the best seafood I've eaten and, of course, Des picked up the tab. Then he ushered us, full of free liquor and free gourmet tucker, into the limousines and said goodnight to us outside our hotel.

Quite apart from his unbelievable hospitality, Des was as nice a guy as you'd wish to meet – and you'd say that even if he wasn't entertaining you royally and paying all the bills. We assumed we'd be seeing him again and a couple of nights later at the official dinner up he bobbed, full of more surprises.

There were 500 people (including our wives) at the dinner and, the understanding was that beer and wines were on the house but spirits drinkers would have to pay for their own. Billy J. Smith was compere for the night and he made that clear in an early announcement.

But our mate Des was having none of that. He stood up and announced that he'd be paying for any spirits anyone wanted to drink, so please sup up heartily. At this rate, he was going to become the most popular man in Australia, and there was more to come.

He also announced that the players' wives – Australian and English – would each receive a $400 voucher good at any Myer store in the country. Do you think he wasn't a hit with the ladies!

Furthermore, he would donate $1000 to the children's hospital cause, main beneficiary of the one-day series, every month for the rest of his life.

I was sitting opposite Rodney Marsh, who had done some advertising work for FAI Insurance, and had got to know Des pretty well while he was in London organising the England players for the Australian trip. "Jesus, 'Bacchus'," I said, "this guy's sensational."

"You're not wrong," said Rodney. "I was having a chat with him this afternoon and I just happened to mention, in passing, that Gary Gilmour was unemployed at the moment.

"He said not to worry, to tell Gary he was on the FAI payroll as from midnight tonight!"

You don't meet guys like Des very often, I can tell you. And that's a great pity in more ways than one.

One of the highlights of the 'senior cits' series was the television coverage by the Nine Network. For the first time in this country, and probably anywhere in the world, players wore microphones on the field. It gave cricket a new dimension.

Max Walker, Rodney Marsh, Tony Greig and Bob Willis were 'wired for sound' and their comments, backwards and forwards among themselves and to the commentary box, gave the coverage an enormous lift.

The reaction I heard during and after was all good, and the obvious question was asked: "Why don't they do this in all forms of televised cricket?"

Well, for the obvious reason that it would create a considerable language – bad language – problem. I can imagine outraged viewers swamping the Nine switchboard after a tense on-field situation in a Test match. Just as you can't teach old dogs new tricks, you can't teach old cricketers to substitute 'damn' for the more traditional four-letter word in the heat of battle. And who ever heard of R-rated cricket telecasts?

I did a session in the commentary box during the Brisbane game when Greig was bowling to David Hookes. Remembering their celebrated confrontation in the Centenary Test more than 10 years earlier, I said: "You're in a bit of trouble here, Tony. How are you going to bowl to David this time?" Tony's reply came straight back on air – the type of stuff that makes for excellent TV.

Hookes was the star of that match and was on 95, with Australia needing one run to win, as Tony started the last over. David badly wanted to end the game with a six to complete his century and from the commentary box, Bill Lawry bet Tony $10 (to go to the children's hospital fund) that he'd do it.

David threw the bat at the first ball but got it only as far as deep mid-off and refused to run what would have been a very comfortable single. The $10 wager was promptly doubled. David attacked the next ball and managed to hole out, also to deep mid-off.

So Tony had the last laugh and he couldn't resist a parting on-air shot at 'Phantom'.

"You're $20 out of pocket now, Bill," he said. "I suppose your pigeons will have to starve for the next couple of weeks."

The Australian oldies beat the England geriatrics 3-0 and made it a truly clean sweep by even cleaning them up at golf in a charity event at Brisbane's Indooroopilly course. A lot of Brisbane rugby league stars were playing that day and Wally Lewis, who is a real football identity up there, excelled himself on the first tee.

The driver slipped from his hands on the follow-through and splashed into the middle of a lake to the left of the tee. It was not unlike that shot I played at Royal Bombay in 1969.

Wally played on without his driver but paused at the halfway mark to tell the resident pro about his unfortunate experience with the water hazard.

"What do want me to do about it, Wally?" asked the pro. "If you think I'm going swimming to retrieve your club, you're crazy."

"That's okay," said Wally, "I'm just warning you, that's all. If I walk into your pro shop next week and my club's up on the wall with a 'for sale' tag on it, there's going to be trouble!"

The cricket series itself was a major success on all counts. From a charity viewpoint, it was a bonanza for hospitalised kids; I know the players had a great time on and off the field; and the games were certainly well received by the public.

It led to suggestions that similar veterans' series be played on a regular basis. Tell you what: they wouldn't want to be *too* regular; not for Doug Walters. I don't think the body would stand up to it. Still, the idea is worth considering.

The muscles started to complain after the first game and slowed a lot of the guys down for the second and third. The Poms seemed to suffer more than we did, although our Gary Gilmour suffered most of all. We did a fair bit of drinking and exotic eating during the 10 or 11 days we were together – and that's exactly what Gary's gout condition didn't need. We ribbed the hell out of him, but I know he was in considerable pain a lot of the time.

Gout sufferers get very little sympathy.

The outstanding performers for Australia were David Hookes, who had a bit of youth and match fitness on his side, Gary Cosier, who hit the ball very well in Adelaide, and Greg Chappell, who looked as if he'd never had a bat out of his hand in retirement.

I thought the respective wicketkeepers, Marshie and Bob Taylor, did great jobs and that Maxie Walker was our best bowler. I suspect 'Tangles' had been doing a spot of secret training. He'd lost very little of the old ability in those years away from active service – and he certainly hadn't lost any of his cheek.

Maxie always enjoyed having a crack at umpires wherever he played, and he showed in the Brisbane match that nothing had changed.

He apologised to umpire Mel Johnson at one stage after a half-hearted and obviously-frivolous appeal for leg-before had been turned down. "Sorry, Mel," he said, "that was silly of me. Quite clearly, he wasn't out and and it was stupid of me to appeal. I won't waste your time by appealing again unless he's definitely out."

Mel smiled and said that would be a very good idea. Maxie's very next ball struck the pad a good 18 inches outside the line of leg stump. And what did he do? He went up for the biggest appeal of all time!

Mel did his very best to look stern. He couldn't. He broke up.

For me, the real highlight of the series was the mateship, the end of the 'cold war', if you like, as I'd known it between Australian and England cricketing camps. I'd always thought the rivalry between those camps had perhaps been taken to unnecessary lengths. Everyone likes to win, sure; but it had never been the end of my world when I didn't.

It was a treat to meet the Poms – yesterday's deadly enemy – in a non-war situation; a treat to have a few beers and a few genuine laughs with them.

It was a very refreshing change.

21

WHEN BILLY BAILED OUT

Billy Watson opened the batting for NSW and Australia before I made the first-class scene. He went by the nickname 'Blinks', and although he may have constantly blinked as opposing fast bowlers sent down their thunderbolts at him, it took a lightning flash to make him actually flinch. And when Billy flinched, he bolted!

A storm was brewing late one afternoon as Billy opened the batting at the SCG for NSW against South Australia. Heavy black clouds had accumulated and an early finish to the day's play seemed inevitable. Still, until the heavens opened, the show must go on.

The bowler bore in with head down and he'd just started his run to unleash the first ball of the innings when lightning split the sky. When he lifted his head just short of the delivery stride he did a double-take – there was an empty crease at the other end! He aborted the delivery and surveyed the field in time to see 'Blinks' disappearing through the gate into the members' stand.

NSW captain Richie Benaud, who had watched from the dressing room as Watson made his amazing retreat, met him inside the gate. 'Blinks,' he said, "what the hell do you think you're doing?" Or words to that effect, but perhaps a little stronger.

"Richie," said Blinks, "you've heard of the writing on the wall. Well, I just saw it in the sky.

"That wasn't sheet lightning it was bloody chain lightning and it said 'WW' in large flashing lights.

"If I go back out there again I'm a goner. I'm not bloody going."

Watson's revolt raised a number of potential problems, particularly for the official scorers. How would they record his departure? Retired hurt or retired terrified, or even run out out by an act of God?

The storm which had started it all settled it by breaking in bucketsful and winding up play for the day. And there in the NSW room was Billy Watson, loudly applauding the deluge and shouting things like, "Send her down, Hughie!"

22

SPUN OUT!

You learn a lot sitting up there in the Channel Nine commentary box describing a game of cricket. One of my earliest lessons was that you don't ask Richie Benaud to answer hypothetical questions on air.

Nine invited me in 1987 to do some commentary work and one of my first assignments was the SCG Test between Australia and England. I was very much a rookie at this business and I thought the best way to make the big impression and show off my wisdom might be to come up with an incisive question at the right moment and develop it into a talking point.

I was on air with Richie and the wicket was obviously taking spin. Here, then, was just the opening I needed.

"Richie," I said, "it seems to me that this is just the type of wicket you'd have enjoyed bowling on."

Good one, I thought. Richie would now say something like, "Indeed, Doug. I think any spin bowler would like to be out there at the moment". This would develop into a meaningful discussion and eliminate those pauses which, at that fledgling stage of my commentating career, were my biggest worry.

Unfortunately, Richie responded with total silence. Not a word. I assumed he hadn't heard me.

"Richie," I said (a little louder this time), "I think you would have enjoyed bowling on this type of wicket."

He turned his head, gave me a little grin and looked straight back at the cricket. I changed the subject and decided that Richie Benaud wasn't one for hypothetical questions, particularly if they are about himself. He called it as it was – which probably accounts for the fact that he is the best cricket commentator in the world today.

23

THE GREATEST!

I'm asked so often to nominate the best batsman, bowler, all-rounder and wicketkeeper of my time that I'm sometimes tempted to answer 'Doug Walters' to all four questions. Purely as a gag, you understand, or as a lazy man's way out of an interrogation I've been through a few hundred times before.

Then I think that if people are interested enough in my thoughts on the game to ask the questions, I at least owe them the courtesy of a serious, honest reply. My answer usually goes like this, not necessarily in the order of asking:

I start off with the ideal cricketer, the incomparable all-rounder, and that unquestionably was Gary Sobers. There was nothing he couldn't do on the cricket field. He was a magnificent batsman, an ever-dangerous medium-pace or spin bowler, a superb fieldsman and a shrewd, attacking captain. He had the lot. They say he was the best all-rounder ever and I don't doubt it, although I'm not quite old enough to personally pass judgement on all those who preceded him. Certainly there was no-one in my era to approach him.

I also rate Sobers as the best batsman of my experience. Hey, you might say, what about Viv Richards? What about Greg and Ian Chappell? What about Barry

Richards and Graeme Pollock? If you said that, you'd have a case and if you took me back through the individual performances of each, you might catch me out on pure statistics.

But I'd still say Sobers. He was complete. He was technically correct, but innovative at the same time. And my, couldn't he punish a ball with such effortless grace! I guess that's what set him apart – he made everything look so easy. He had so much time to play his shots, even against express pace, that you half-expected him to stifle a yawn between the moment of delivery and the moment of contact with the bat. I group together, just marginally below Sobers, the other batsmen I have named. Viv Richards is known as the Black Bradman and, on his day, is indeed capable of Bradman-like deeds. But I make a point of 'on his day'. Richards was, and still is, a super batsman, but you tread on dangerous ground when you start to compare him, even broadly, with Bradman.

The Chappell brothers were certainly the two best Australian batsmen of my playing time and, really, I can't split them. If you had to toss a coin for them, you wouldn't mind which side it came down. They were different types – Greg the stylist, Ian the more belligerent hitter of the ball. Under all conditions, maybe Ian. But I prefer to call it a dead-heat.

I didn't see enough of Barry Richards or Pollock to set them above my other nominations. Let's face it, no-one outside South Africa saw nearly enough of them. It is one of the game's great pities that politics deprived international cricket of their great talents.

The bowlers must be categorised according to their pace, but Dennis Lillee was the best – fast, medium or slow – I played with or against. I played against him too

IT WAS BAD ENOUGH FACING HIM IN THE NETS !

often for my liking. Two Sheffield Shield matches a season against Western Australia were two too many when you had Dennis charging in and whipping the ball around your ears at high speed. It was bad enough facing him in the nets – and I was a mate. Imagine shaping up to him in a Test arena if he didn't particularly like you!

Excluding Dennis, I regard Jeff Thomson and West Indians Wesley Hall and Michael Holding as the best of the pacemen. Again, it's a bit of a toss-up, but I saw a lot of 'Thommo' at his peak, before he injured his shoulder, and I give him the nod.

Jeff was a brute of a bowler. He wasn't particularly accurate, but that just made him all the more lethal. You knew he was going to put at least a couple of balls an over on the spot and all you could do was wait for them. Then again, you didn't know if his lethal ball was going to be a sandshoe-crusher or a cranium-cracker. It was a dodgy business – literally – facing Jeff Thomson.

My votes in the slow-bowling department go to England's Derek Underwood and Indian Bishen Bedi, in that order. They were left-arm orthodox spinners and their type of bowling gave me more trouble than any other. I lean towards Underwood because of his ability to whip the ball through and spin it at the same time. It made him a particularly difficult customer.

Which leaves the wicketkeepers. Three stand out – Wally Grout, Alan Knott and Rodney Marsh. Great glovemen all and I can't separate them. Grout was a street ahead of any other Australian keeper of his vintage, Knott was totally professional and wouldn't let the flies through and Marshie holds the world record for dismissals behind the stumps.

I agree with the consensus that the Englishman kept better to spin, but he had a lot more experience at that, didn't he? Given the same experience, I think Rodney would have topped the list – and that's not just mateship talking. As it is, I bracket the three.

So there you have them – Doug's Devastating Dozen-or-so. Friend or foe, it was a great privilege to have rubbed shoulders or locked horns with them in the greatest game in the world.

I look forward, in years to come, to telling my grandkids all about it.

24

BAPTISM OF FIRE

Richie Benaud's act was always going to be too hard for younger brother John to follow. That's no disgrace because Richie's contribution to Australian cricket has been quite unique on and off the field.

It's fair to say, I think, that John Benaud lived in his big brother's shadow, but that didn't stop him deciding that he was going to play cricket for his country, too.

And that he did. His international career was brief. He didn't play many games, but I'll bet he never forgets his first.

It was against the Rest of the World at Adelaide Oval in 1970 and the team had assembled early for slips-catching practice. Being a rookie, John was very nervous. He'd taken up smoking only a couple of weeks earlier and he was really giving the cigarettes a hiding as he anticipated his debut.

John had been given the locker next to Dennis Lillee, that extroverted king of speed and swing, who arrived toting a brand-new, shiny green, plastic gear bag of which he was justifiably proud. Loving wife Helen had packed his finest and newly-pressed creams into it and Dennis reckoned he was going to be the best-equipped bloke in the ball-game.

He put his bag on the floor below his locker. Benaud produced a book of matches to light yet another cigarette and, deep in thought, flicked the match idly away.

When we returned from fielding practice half an hour later, the dressing room was full of smoke. And the source of it was Dennis' smart new bag.

Without actually setting fire to it, John's match had managed to smoulder its way through the bag's total contents – creams, socks, jockstrap and all. It was just starting on the bottom of the bag itself.

What does a new chum say to a bloke like Dennis Lillee when he's just burned holes in a complete set of gear? Very little.

He spluttered something like, "Christ, I'm sorry", but the apology tended to be lost amid Dennis' outrage.

No, John Benaud won't forget his debut for his country – the day he damned near sent Adelaide Oval up in smoke!

THE DRESSING ROOM WAS FULL OF SMOKE!

25

ENTER MAX – RIGHT ON CUE!

I should point out right from the start here that I am *not* a dab hand on the billiard table. Billiards, snooker, pool... you name it and I'm ordinary at it. Less than ordinary, I suppose.

I know a lot of cricketers, past and present, who wield a mean cue. Batsmen, particularly, often excel on the green sward and I guess it all has to do with the eye. But whenever I saw a red ball, I wanted to hook it, cut it, or drive it back past the bowler. Poking it into a pocket with a white ball on the end of a long stick never appealed to me much. I like to think of my attitude as evidence of a constructively-spent youth.

Still, even a no-talent potter should feel pretty secure when his partner in a four-handed game of snooker is Cliff Thorburn, Canadian professional champion who, when our paths crossed, was on his way to becoming the best exponent of his craft in the world, officially.

Cliff and I teamed up, with the most unexpected results, against a couple of 'mugs' one night in the billiard room of Sydney's Muirfield North Rocks Golf Club.

The adventure had started the previous day over beers at the Bridge Hotel in Rozelle. Cliff was in town for a major tournament, and, my old mate Brian Taber and I were showing him, and his English colleague John Pulman, a little traditional Aussie hospitality.

The talk got around to golf eventually and Cliff mentioned that he would much enjoy a round. No worries, we said, and a hit-off time was promptly arranged for Muirfield early next afternoon. Pulman didn't make it. He wasn't feeling the best when he surfaced in the morning and declared himself a late scratching. His place was taken at short notice by Peter Spence, an outstanding junior cricket coach who has done great things for the game in NSW.

The round was played amid a certain amount of hilarity and, of course, a drink was compulsory at the 19th hole. It was more than one drink, actually, and when they announced at 8 pm that the bar was about to close, Cliff suggested we take a couple of jugs into the billiard room – which he'd inspected as a matter of professional interest – and play a game of snooker.

Taber said he would have to give that a miss because he was expected home, so we rang in a club member, Max, to make up the four.

We tossed for partners, and I just happened to draw Cliff (whom we'd introduced to Max only by Christian name). And we agreed that the stake would be a lottery ticket a corner.

Whichever way the coin had come down in the draw for partners, it was clearly going to be a mismatch. I mean, Cliff could have taken us all on, blindfolded and with a stick of cabana for a cue, and beaten the pants off us. So we got together, the champ and I, and agreed that we (or he) should stretch it out into a black-ball game. Just to make it interesting, you see.

Well, Cliff managed to restrain his extraordinary talents without making it look too obvious, and it got down to the pink and the black – and my shot. The pink was sitting over a corner pocket and the black was safe

DID I MENTION THAT I'M NO GREAT SHAKES AT
THESE INDOOR BALL GAMES !

enough, up against the cushion halfway between centre and corner.

No worries here, I thought. What I'll do is pot the pink – anyone could pot it from that position – and leave the black safe for Cliff to finish off after Max fails.

Did I mention that I'm no great shakes at these indoor ball games? I had an air-shot on the pink! Missed it completely. That was bad enough, but worse still was that the cue ball came back, dislodged the black from the cushion and left it over a centre pocket.

It was easy meat for Max, who potted both balls with ease and beamed broadly.

Game over, and a little still left in the last jug, Cliff treated us to a few of his trick shots. He did some amazing things. He jumped balls, he swerved around them. He damn near made them talk.

It was all too much for Max, who could imagine the club's precious cloth being ripped down the middle by this 'show-off with the accent'.

"Hey, steady on, mate," he said. "You'll tear the bloody table. You mightn't know it, but that cloth costs a lot of money!"

Cliff shrugged at Max, winked at me, and we all went home.

I was back at Muirfield next day with Max's lottery ticket.

"Do you realise," I said, "that the bloke you played against last night was Cliff Thorburn, the Canadian professional snooker champion?"

It took a lot to impress Max, and probably still does.

"I don't care if he was Walter Lindrum," he said. "It cost him a lottery ticket to find out how good I am!"

Cliff Thorburn won the world championship that very year.

Nice one, Max!

127

26

OUR BELOVED LEADER

Ian Chappell was the best captain I played with or against. He was a great cricketer himself and he understood players, their moods and their problems better than any other skipper I've known.

Before the start of a tour, 'Chappelli' would get the boys together, tell them what lay ahead and what was expected of them, and, assure them that his door was always open. It was, too – a fact that some of us would maybe abuse a little on our way upstairs from bars in various hotels around the world. Nothing too outrageous, generally just a chat and a nightcap with our beloved leader.

The open door policy very nearly got me sent home in disgrace from our 1969 tour of India. In this case, Ian's door wasn't open – but manager Fred Bennett's was.

Ian and I left the bar of our Delhi hotel pretty late one night (or pretty early one morning) and on the way upstairs I suggested a cup of coffee before bed. When he said "fine", I volunteered to make it and, having done so, walked across the corridor to Ian's room to tell him it was ready.

The doorbells in that hotel had a ring like a fire alarm and I was still leaning on Ian's when Fred Bennett emerged, sleepy-eyed, pyjama-clad and none too happy,

THE DOORBELLS IN THAT HOTEL HAD A RING LIKE A
FIRE ALARM !

from his room next door. What the hell was going on he
demanded, and tended to doubt me when I said the
skipper and I were going to have a cup of coffee before
we hit the sack.

"Nonsense," said Fred, "Ian wouldn't be up at this
hour of the night. Now you go to bed!"

"Bullshit, Fred," said I. "Look, I'll bet he's in there
listening through the keyhole to every word we're
saying."

129

We had a nice old row out there in the corridor and Fred came the heavy by threatening to send me back to Australia on the next flight.

I was cheeky enough to call his bluff. In fact, I begged him to do it. He didn't – but I couldn't help but wonder next day when I remembered that Ian didn't drink coffee (or tea) and never had. I suspected he'd tried to give Doug Walters the slip and get to bed before the roosters of Delhi started crowing.

Only once did I really run foul of Ian Chappell's captaincy – and that again had to do with a late night.

I had a terribly difficult decision to make in Kingston, Jamaica, during the 1973 tour of the West Indies. Should I go along to the Rothmans ball on the Friday night? Or should I give it a miss and wake up clear of eye and sweet of breath for the start of the First Test the following morning. I did what any invited, conscientious Rothmans' employee would do. I went to the ball.

It was well after Cinderella's deadline when I got back to the hotel but Terry Jenner, with whom I was rooming, had told me he was getting up extra early to do some shopping before the game and he'd arrange for the hotel desk to give me a call an hour after he left. To make doubly sure, he would order my breakfast as well.

I heard Terry's early-morning reminder call come through, and promptly went back to sleep. The next call was at 10.55 a.m. – five minutes before the start of play. It was Terry in the dressing room at the ground, Sabina Park. Christ, he said, what happened? You'd better get yourself down here in a hurry. 'Chappelli's' asking questions.

The shower-and-dressing operation was achieved in world record time and I managed to trip over my breakfast – sitting there cold on its tray in the middle of the floor – as I fled the room. They might have told me!

My luck changed as I left the motel because there was a taxi on the rank outside, the driver recognised me and, being a West Indian and therefore a cricket fanatic, knew where I should have been at that very moment.

Talk about your nightmare drives! Sabina Park was about five miles from the hotel and the traffic would

WE TRAVELLED A GOOD DEAL OF THE JOURNEY ON THE FOOTPATH!

have made peak hour in Sydney look like a public holiday in a ghost town. We travelled a good deal of the journey on the footpath, but such was the cabbie's skill that the game was only three overs old when we reached the ground.

John Benaud was 12th man and I stood at the boundary gate waving and saying "I'm here – I'm here." The response from the field must have been pre-arranged. They totally ignored me. I stood there like an idiot and let another over pass, then decided this had gone far enough. So I strode on to the field and Benaud duly walked off.

Ian Chappell gave me a look which told me I wasn't No. 1 on his Lovable Chaps List, pointed to the fine-leg boundary and said: "Down there, you!" So down there I went.

At the end of the over, he pointed to the third-man boundary, at the other end of the ground, and said: "Down there, you!"

For the rest of the session, I alternated between fine-leg and third man – and you don't have to be a cricket buff to know that these are far-flung fielding positions. By lunch, I'd covered more ground than Cliffy Young and I was looking for a place to lie down.

As we left the field, Chappelli said, ever so quickly but with unmistakable authority: "That'll never happen again, will it?"

"I can't promise you," I replied, "but I hope it doesn't."

It didn't – but if you think I was a little late that day, let me tell you about John Inverarity during the 1968 tour of England. Invers was so late for the first day of our three-day match against Minor Counties that he damn near didn't make it at all. And the captain, Bill Lawry this time, didn't even know he was missing.

The game was at Torquay and we stayed at a motel-casino complex directly opposite the ground. There was no need for a roll call here, no need to count heads as they popped out of taxis. If you couldn't find your way across the street to get to this ground on time, you were beyond help.

We'd been in the field for three-quarters of an hour when Ian Chappell drew my attention to the fact that we were a man short. "Do you notice there's someone missing around here?" he asked as our paths crossed between overs.

I did a quick count and, sure enough, there were only 10 of us out there. A deeper analysis revealed that we were light on by one John Inverarity.

It was fast approaching lunch by the time Invers appeared. He came in by the back gate, walked along the perimeter of the arena and managed to mingle so quickly and unobtrusively with the rest of the field that Lawry thought he'd been there from the outset. He was unaware of the shortfall until 'Chappelli' mentioned it in passing many years later.

Funny, really, because as a skipper, Bill was always a stickler for detail out there on the field. I reckon he ran out of fingers when he was counting his troops that day.

Ian Chappell's particular way of dishing out discipline had a profound effect on Bob Massie. 'Chappelli' was no angel himself, of course, and the very last thing you'd call him is a hypocrite.

To publicly – even privately – read the riot act to an errant player was not his style at all. He struck a nice compromise between being leader of the boys and being one of them. If you stepped out of line off the field, you paid for it on the field next day.

Bob Massie discovered that during that 1973 tour of the West Indies. 'Fergie' – he derived the nickname from the Massey-Ferguson association of words rather than any connection with future royalty – took me on at the bar on the eve of our three-day game against Leeward Islands. He was drinking rum-and-Coke. So was his mate and accomplice Terry Jenner. I was drinking beer.

Bob and Terry did very well for a while and even when they were dancing about on one leg apiece like a couple of itchy-footed brolgas, they were keeping the barmaid busy. I like a rum myself and there's no shortage of it in the Caribbean, I can tell you. But they really gave it a belt that night.

Terry was first to hit the surrender button and 'Fergie' called it a night after a few more rums than he needed. He somehow made it back to his room and began a long, losing battle to get his trousers off. Getting them down was easy enough, but getting them off over his shoes – which he hadn't thought to remove – was not even a possibility in the standing or stooped position.

The performance was watched with fascinated amusement by his room-mate, John Benaud.

"You certainly had to admire Fergie's tenacity," John told us later. "Every time he bent down to get his pants off, he fell over. Eventually, he laid on the bed, stuck his legs in the air and tried it that way."

It was great live entertainment, 'Benords' reckoned, but it was turning into a late, late show and he thought Fergie had suffered enough – so he took off his shoes and trousers and put him under the covers.

'Chappelli' approached John at the ground next morning. "What did you do to 'Fergie' last night?" he demanded. "He's still pissed!"

"Nothing, skip," said John. "I just tucked him in."

After we'd batted first and made only 191 against those West Indies quicks who just love to bowl first, out we went to field. Viv Richards, young, but already with a big reputation, was at No. 5 for the Leewards.

So out we went. And 'Chappelli' invited (well, instructed) 'Fergie' to open the attack. The ball was tossed to Bob and he actually caught it, which wasn't bad for a bloke who hadn't been able to get his daks off a few hours earlier and was still breathing heavy molasses' fumes.

By this stage, Ian had obviously ferreted out the fact that Terry Jenner had taken a few rums last night as well. He figured it would be nice for Terry to be involved in the action, so he put him at mid-on.

'Fergie's' first ball was a wide, shoulder-high full toss which the astonished batsman flung a late bat at and missed very comfortably. The second and third were of very similar line and length and also defied the batsman's valiant attempts at contact.

The fourth delivery was virtually a replica of its predecessors – but the batsman had grown almost accustomed by now to this extraordinary performance and was lying in wait. He lunged at the ball but managed only to dolly it straight to mid-on. There, standing in his own little fog, was Terry Jenner, who saw the ball so late he barely managed to get a hand to it before grassing the easiest of catches.

And if you think Terry's judgement was impaired, consider poor 'Fergie'. He hadn't seen the ball at all after delivery and was still scanning the field for it when Terry handed it back and apologised for dropping the catch.

"Don't worry," said Bob. "Didn't realise it had gone in the air. Sun was in my eyes."

There was to be little respite for 'Fergie' in that opening session. 'Chappelli' kept him on for what must have been the most painful hour of his cricketing career and had him patrolling the fine-leg fence between overs.

His fielding was reasonably good, without much work coming his way, until Viv Richards glanced one very sweetly.

'Fergie's' fuzzy mind raced back to basics, to the coach who'd told him at junior level to drop a knee behind the ball in case it slipped through the hands.

So he propped, dropped to one knee in copybook junior fashion, cupped the hands at ground level . . . and waited.

He was still waiting in that classical pose when the ball crossed the boundary line five yards to his right!

The expression on 'Chappelli's' face covered many emotions, but I guess an equal mix of horror and amusement overrode all others.

Ian had a word with 'Fergie' as we left the field for lunch. "Hope you learned something out there this morning." he said. 'Fergie' thought for just a moment and replied: "Yeah. Coke affects your sense of direction."